Doing Your Undergraduate Social Science Dissertation

Are you a final-year social science student who has to do a dissertation or final-year project?

Do you have no idea where to start?

If so, *Doing Your Undergraduate Social Science Dissertation* is the book for you, covering the whole dissertation journey from project planning to submission. Using a mixture of useful information, exercises, practical strategies, case study material and further reading, it helps you through the process, giving hints and tips on beginning and managing your research project and working with your supervisors. Packed with proven practical advice, it also identifies many other sources of information and resources, making it your most dependable starting point and guide on your dissertation journey. Also included are links to accompanying materials on the Routledge website.

The authors have extensive experience in teaching at all levels in the social sciences, supervising social science undergraduates and dissertations.

Karen Smith is Research Fellow at Glasgow Caledonian University.

Malcolm Todd is Senior Academic at Sheffield Hallam University, where he is Head of Learning and Teaching for the Faculty of Development and Society.

Julia Waldman is Principal Research Officer at the National Foundation for Educational Research, the UK's largest independent educational research organization.

Doing Your Undergraduate Social Science Dissertation

Karen Smith, Malcolm Todd
and Julia Waldman

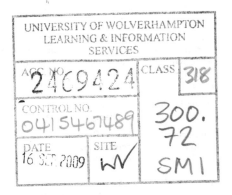
Routledge
Taylor & Francis Group

LONDON AND NEW YORK

First published 2009
by Routledge
2 Park Square, Milton Park, Abingdon, Oxon OX14 4RN

Simultaneously published in the USA and Canada
by Routledge
270 Madison Ave, New York, NY 10016

Routledge is an imprint of the Taylor & Francis Group, an informa business

© 2009 Karen Smith, Malcolm Todd and Julia Waldman

Typeset in Garamond by
Wearset Ltd, Boldon, Tyne and Wear
Printed and bound in Great Britain by
TJ International Ltd, Padstow, Cornwall

British Library Cataloguing in Publication Data
A catalogue record for this book is available from the British Library

Library of Congress Cataloging-in-Publication Data
  Doing your undergraduate social science dissertation /
Karen Smith, Malcolm Todd, and Julia Waldman.
     p. cm.
  Includes bibliographical references and index.
  1. Dissertations, Academic. 2. Social sciences—Research—
Methodology. I. Todd, Malcolm J. II. Waldman, Julia. III. Title.
  LB2369.S613 2009
  300.7'2—dc22   2008038500

ISBN10: 0-415-46748-9 (hbk)
ISBN10: 0-415-46749-7 (pbk)
ISBN10: 0-203-88126-5 (ebk)

ISBN13: 978-0-415-46748-3 (hbk)
ISBN13: 978-0-415-46749-0 (pbk)
ISBN13: 978-0-203-88126-2 (ebk)

This book is for the three pillars that hold me up: my parents, Jean and Colin, and my husband Chidochangu.
Karen Smith

I would like to thank my wife Sally for her patience and support throughout the production of this book and for taking on more than her share of childcare duties. I would like to dedicate this book to my daughters Isobel and Imogen and to my mother Ivy.
Malcolm Todd

Dedicated with love and thanks to my accepting husband Keith and to each of my amazing children Jamie, Holly, Robin and Ryan.
Julia Waldman

Contents

Illustrations

Figures

Tables

Preface

As undergraduate social science students, for many of you a significant part of your final-year study at college or university will focus on an independent learning project. The name for this project may vary from institution to institution and from country to country: in some places, in the UK, for example, it could be called a 'dissertation'; elsewhere it could be described as an 'extended essay' or 'final-year project'. Whichever way your own institution describes it, we are aware that the dissertation can demand a great deal from you in (synthesizing theory, selecting and applying methodology, conducting research and analysing data, etc.) and that many of you may not feel fully prepared for this form of assessment. We have tried, therefore, to write a book for you in an approachable and accessible style, one that provides you with support and guidance to help you through the dissertation process.

Our aims

When setting out to write *Doing Your Undergraduate Social Science Dissertation*, we had three main aims. First, we intended the book to be one that you use often. This may seem an obvious statement, but we wanted to provide you with a source book that was able to respond to some of the frequent questions, concerns and practical issues you come across when preparing for and completing your dissertation or final-year project. We and the many contributors to this book have themselves had extensive experience in teaching at all levels in the social sciences, in supervising many social science undergraduate students and in doing dissertations. So, the book is informed by our own extensive collective practice as supervisors of dissertation students.

A second fundamental aim of the book is that it should be informed not only by our own experience but also by research and evidence. Two of the authors have had a long-standing research interest in exploring the experiences and perceptions of final-year social science undergraduates enrolled on dissertation modules in the UK and in Hong Kong. They have also researched the staff experience of supervising final-year students, have published findings in international learning and teaching journals and have presented work around the world on these issues. All three authors have a long-standing and wide research interest in understanding how students learn and how, as teachers, they can look at ways of supporting students to achieve their own full potential. You will see that in many of the chapters in this book we will cite evidence from research and studies into student learning. The book is, thus, also informed by a research and evidence base.

Third, the book takes a strongly student-centred stance. We did not believe we could, or would want to, write a book with the aim of providing you with a set of definitive answers about producing a dissertation or final-year project; instead, we recognize that there are many ways in which the 'journey' through the process can be completed. We felt that this book should be a dependable resource that is a starting point for you on your dissertation journey. The book should be supplemented by discussions with your tutors, your fellow students and information provided by your university. In addition, there are many other resources and sources of information which you can and should access, some of which we identify in our bibliography and on our accompanying website. We believe that students should aim to become effective, independent and self-confident learners, who can make informed decisions about their own learning. We strongly believe that this is a key characteristic of becoming an autonomous learner, and we hope that the book will contribute in some small way to that aim. Importantly, we want to help you have success in your dissertation and hope this book will help achieve this.

How to use this book

It is intended that the book should be useful in the preparation period when you're thinking about the focus of your dissertation, research design, collection of data and their analysis, and throughout your final year – right up to submitting the final project and what happens afterwards. The chapters will follow a sequence that is designed to help you through a number of these key stages. But we have also designed the book so it can be used in a more flexible way and be adaptable as your own needs change. For example, before you start the dissertation, you can use it to:

- explore the demands of a dissertation;
- raise questions that you can ask your supervisor;

- help you think through what theme you could pursue in your dissertation;
- help you prepare a research question.

If you have already started the dissertation, you can also use it to:

- clarify issues about specific chapters of the dissertation;
- focus on specific aspects of the study, e.g. ethical issues or research methodology;
- organize the different stages of the dissertation.

You will see that each chapter contains a number of student and staff reflections and helpful guidance on how to take forward each stage of the process. There will be a series of case studies which we hope will provide a helpful way for you to better understand your own progress on the dissertation journey. Each chapter concludes with a set of key messages and key questions. These are provided to assist you with reflecting upon what you have gained from each chapter and what action you may need to take your own dissertation forward.

Concluding comments

The web pages that accompany this book contain additional useful supplementary information and material such as links to relevant web resources. It is accessible from the publisher's website. We hope that this book will offer you some practical support along your learning journey, and we welcome feedback from you on how we might be able to improve future editions of this book.

Note: Comments in grey boxes are reflections and tips provided by students and staff.

Acknowledgements

This book has grown out of an online resource, *The Companion for Undergraduate Dissertations*, developed by Malcolm Todd and Julia Waldman and the Higher Education Academy's Subject Centres for Sociology, Anthropology and Politics (C-SAP) and Social Work and Policy (SWAP) and including the contributions of many other contributors. We would like to acknowledge C-SAP and SWAP's ongoing support for our work and in particular that of Helen Howard and Anthony Rosie from C-SAP who made resources available to develop the online support and Jackie Rafferty of SWAP.

We would also like to recognize the contributions of Ian Baker (Chapters 2, 3, 5 and 10), Jenny Blain (3 and 5), Sue Hemmings (3), Anne Hollows (2, 3 and 10), Ann Macaskill (7), Darren Marsh (11), Ruth McManus (7), Liam Mellor (2), Janet Morton (4), Andy Pilkington (10), Gary Taylor (2), John Steel (10) and Christopher Winch (5 and 10). Their work, which originally appeared in *The Companion*, has helped to shape much of this book.

Thank you also to the following people for contributing many of the insightful quotes and case studies in the book: Mike Bracher, Iain Garner, Caroline Gibson, Marcus Green, Catherine Hanley, Katherine Harrington, Cath Lambert, Sarah Lynch, Tsang Kwok Kuen, David Metcalfe, Peter O'Neill, Gillian Ruch, Beverley Searle, Becky Webb and Kanishka Wattage and Alan McGauley.

We are also indebted to the critical friends who gave us insightful feedback on draft chapters of this book. They are: Sean Demack, Scott Fernie, Carol Hayden, Jessica Henderson, Martina Johnson, Liz Lawrence, Colin McCaig, Darren Marsh, Marian Morris, Nick Pilcher, Jackie Powell, Steve Spencer, Viv Thom, Cal Weatherald and Rose Wiles.

Thank you also to Liz O'Donnell, our proof reader and the editorial team at Routledge: Philip Mudd, Alistair Shaw and Lucy Wainwright.

We would like to thank Carfax Publishing Company, part of the Taylor & Francis Group for permission to cite from: Todd, M., Bannister, P. and Clegg, S. 'Independent inquiry and the undergraduate dissertation: perceptions and experiences of final-year social science students', *Assessment and Evaluation in Higher Education*, 29 (3) June 2004. We would also like to thank Routledge for permission to cite from: Todd, M.J., Smith, K. and Bannister, P. 'Staff Experiences and Perceptions of Supervising a Social Science Undergraduate Dissertation', *Teaching in Higher Education*, 11 (2) 2006.

But our biggest thanks go to our social science dissertation students whose experiences motivated us to write this book.

Image reproduced in Chapter 5 included with the kind permission of Robin Waldman.

Figure 12.1 produced in Chapter 12 reproduced with the kind permission of the Quality Assurance Agency (QAA).

Chapter 1

What is a dissertation?

Introduction

This chapter explores what a dissertation or final-year project is in order to better understand the distinctive features of this form of assessment within your degree programme. It highlights the ways in which the dissertation differs from other modules you may be taking or be about to undertake and the expectations it places on you, the learner, to take responsibility for your own learning. By the end of this chapter, you should have a better understanding of the following:

- what a dissertation is;
- what makes the dissertation special;
- what your dissertation may look like;
- how to prepare for the dissertation.

Definitions of the dissertation

For many undergraduate social science degree students, a significant element of final-year study is an independent learning project. In this book we call the project a 'dissertation', but other terms, including 'extended essay', 'independent learning project', 'capstone project', 'senior paper' or 'final-year project' are also used.

While these projects may vary greatly in scope and nature (e.g. a large-scale written assignment such as a dissertation or extended essay or the design and production of some type of artefact), most share a number of key characteristics (Todd *et al.* 2004):

1   The learner determines the focus and direction of their work.
2   This work is carried out on an individual basis – although usually with some tutor support and direction provided.

3 There is typically a substantial research component to the project, requiring the collection of primary data, the analysis of existing/secondary data or both.

4 Learners will have a more prolonged engagement with the chosen subject than is the case with 'standard' coursework assignments such as essays or reports, with the work consequently expected to be more in-depth.

What distinguishes the dissertation?

The dissertation offers you the opportunity to further develop your subject expertise and your social research, intellectual and organizational skills. The dissertation requires becoming actively involved with research. This could mean empirical research or a library-based project. It provides more opportunity for originality and intellectual independence than you have perhaps experienced before.

Your first essays were usually (though not always) written to titles that had been prescribed by your tutor. As you progressed through your course, you may have been given the opportunity to make up your own titles. In this way your independence, as a reader and critic, developed. Similarly, you may have noticed that you no longer read books and papers simply to understand them and re-present their arguments in an essay. Rather, you notice what particularly interested you in the books, journal articles or media sources and what particular critical questions you wanted to ask about them. The dissertation builds on this foundation; it grows out of your own particular interest, both in terms of the material you choose to write about and the topic that provides the focus of your study.

The longer word count of the dissertation requires you to sustain your analysis and interpretation over a greater range of material and almost inevitably involves you in more careful and subtle argument. The preparation and writing of the dissertation makes you take responsibility, with the support of a tutor, for your own learning. You have to manage your independent study, your time and present the results of research clearly and methodically.

As one student articulated (Todd *et al.* 2004: 339–340):

> In other courses it's set out what they want you to find out. This is about your individual thought and direction – you can go off in your chosen direction, branch out and make different things relate to each other. There's more freedom involved.

In many ways, this is about *doing* social science rather than writing about the social science that others have produced. Some of these skills are clearly academic and related to your discipline. This process improves your subject expertise; it is a good preparation for further study and research at postgraduate level; and it requires you to work independently and methodically in a variety of intellectually demanding contexts. Others are much broader and develop your effectiveness in collecting and manipulating information, presentation and the production of reports critical thinking, problem-solving, and enquiry – all of which will all be beneficial for your professional life.

For these reasons, the dissertation can be seen as the culmination of your undergraduate studies. Here you not only demonstrate the intellectual, study, research and presentation skills that you have developed throughout your degree course, but you also create something which is uniquely your own.

Dissertation organization

The way in which this type of assessment is organized will vary from institution to institution and programme to programme. It is important that you familiarize yourself with the particular arrangements for your degree. Many institutions produce a module handbook setting out these requirements and also allocate students a dissertation tutor or supervisor. Your supervisor, and any handbooks which are produced, are excellent sources of information and support and will help you understand how the dissertation process works.

It is worth being very clear from the earliest planning stages of your dissertation exactly what is being asked of you. Questions that you should be asking yourself include:

- How many credits does the dissertation carry?
- How many words do I have to write?
- How often can I meet my supervisor?
- Are there any interim submission points?

All dissertations will vary in format, style and design. It is important that you familiarize yourself with the particular requirements of your institution and degree programme. A typical dissertation format would look like this:

- Title Page   The title of your dissertation, your name and the name of your supervisor.
- Table of Contents   A detailed list of the chapters (and possibly sub-sections) in your dissertation.
- List of tables and figures (if any)   The titles of any tables or figures (pictures, illustrations or charts) that you have included.
- List of abbreviations (if any), alphabetically ordered   Abbreviations should be spelt out in full. This means that the abbreviations can then be used in the text without further explanation.
- Introduction   This gives a rationale for your research and sets out the structure of your dissertation.
- Literature review   This is similar in form and length to a longish essay entitled 'How I have set up my research topic and how it fits in with existing work in the area.'
- Methodology   Another essay-sized section entitled 'Why I chose the methods I chose to answer my particular question, the strengths and weaknesses of that approach as a tool for generating knowledge, and how I actually did it.'
- Findings   A description and presentation of your own data, evidence or case study. It could be either a certain number of chapters or an extended essay which has clearly identified sections.
- Discussion   This is the section that brings all of the strands of your argument together. One way to think of it is as a three-way conversation between the literature you discussed, the methodology you adopted and the findings you have presented.
- Conclusions and (if appropriate) recommendations   This chapter will draw together the conclusions as well as noting any recommendations for practice. You should not include new ideas at this stage: they should have been dealt with in the discussion section. You can include a reflection on doing the research study and also identify ways in which you, or others, might take the work forward as further research as well as training and dissemination. This chapter often runs out of steam – be warned.
- Bibliography   A list of all the books, journal articles, websites, newspapers and other sources that you have used in your dissertation.
- Appendices   For example, questionnaires, interview transcripts, pilot reports, detailed tables, etc.

The reason why we can confidently suggest that most dissertations will follow this format is that most reporting of research, which is what a dissertation does, carries a very similar shape. Swales *et al.* (2004: 222) describe the dissertation as having four main parts:

1 introductory section;
2 methods;
3 findings;
4 discussion.

The introductory sections begin with a general overview of your research topic. This becomes increasingly specific as you introduce the research questions you are going to pursue, the methods you will use to do that and then the results that those methods give. The dissertation will then become more general again as you relate your specific findings to the wider context. It is useful to imagine a camera. You start with a wide-angled lens which takes in the surrounding environment. Then you focus in closely using the zoom to look in detail at your subject. Then you zoom out again to see the bigger picture.

Preparing for the dissertation

In certain essential ways, what the dissertation reflects is a direct development from the skills that you have acquired through your programme. If you doubt that you have developed during your study, go back and look at one of your first-year assignments and think of improvements you might now be able to make to it.

As you know, when you write a module assessment, you discuss a subject area in relation to a particular idea or topic. The title of your essay, report or examination paper and its first paragraph focus your discussion on the chosen topic and determine the scope of the essay. You undertake a careful reading of a selection of material. Then, within the limits prescribed by the assessment title, you attempt to construct a coherent, closely reasoned and substantiated argument. Your essay does not include all your ideas about the literature area, nor does it attempt to cover every aspect of them. Rather, it makes a particular interpretation. The dissertation may be similarly focused in approach. It identifies a single topic to explore and limits the amount of issues that can be examined in depth and detail within the specified word limit. Initially, then, you will prepare for your dissertation in the same way as you would any written assessment. The key difference is the length and time you have to produce a sustained and justified argument around a topic that you have chosen.

You will also be able to draw upon other experiences, for example, in the analysis and presentation of findings that you may have covered on methodology modules. You are probably aware of where your academic strengths and weaknesses lie. If you have never really thought about this, it would be worth devoting some time to doing so. In setting up your project, you will want to *play to your strengths*. In Chapter 3, we give you more advice on getting started with the dissertation.

Case study: top ten dissertation writing tips

1. Select a topic that interests you

First and foremost, it is crucial that you select a dissertation or project topic that you find interesting. This will provide the initial motivation you need to get started, and it will help you stay engaged and moving forward with your work when time and other pressures begin to surface later on.

2. Know your topic

You should be absolutely clear in your own mind as to what your dissertation or project topic is. Write this down in a couple of sentences and stick it on to your computer. This will help you to know exactly what you need to do and also help prevent you from getting bogged down in material that is irrelevant.

3. Work with your supervisor

Your supervisor is there to provide guidance to enable you to conduct independent research and write your dissertation according to the conventions and expectations of your particular discipline. However, for most students this will be the first experience of working with a lecturer in such a sustained and focused way. It is important that you know what you can expect from your supervisor from the beginning. And it is equally important for you to know what your supervisor expects of you!

4. Seek peer support

Self-organized writing groups with other students can provide a valuable source of support during what is a particularly demanding and sometimes isolating experience of writing at university. Try meeting regularly with a group of peers to discuss your work and any challenges you are facing.

5. Familiarize yourself with the assessment criteria

It is a good idea to find out early what your tutors will be looking for in your dissertation by getting a copy of the assessment criteria and any other guidance provided.

6. Consider the ethical dimension

If your dissertation involves collecting data from human participants, which is most likely to be the case in the sciences or social sciences, you will need to follow your university's ethical guidelines for such work. You are advised to begin considering the ethical dimension of your work as early as possible.

7. Make good use of subject librarians

Subject librarians are an often overlooked but very valuable resource when it comes to dissertation writing. They have specific knowledge of the journals, books and other resources – both printed and online versions – relevant to your particular discipline.

8. Keep track of your sources

From the very beginning of your literature review, it is important you come up with a simple system for keeping track of the complete bibliographic details of what you read. It is especially important to record specific page numbers for any direct quotations you write down when taking notes.

9. Start writing

What can you do when you don't know what or how to start writing? Start writing! One of the best ways to overcome that hurdle of getting started is to give yourself licence to 'freewrite', to simply write down anything that comes to mind on your topic, without stopping, for ten or fifteen minutes. Don't worry about correct spelling or grammar or even writing in complete sentences as freewriting is a creative process.

10. Stay focused

A dissertation is likely to be the longest piece of writing you will complete as an undergraduate, and the risk of straying away from your topic as you progress with your work is much greater than it is with shorter pieces of writing.

(Katherine Harrington and Peter O'Neill, Write Now CETL)

Key messages

- The dissertation is an independent piece of research where you are responsible for your own learning.
- It will demand the use of your communication, information-seeking and intellectual skills.
- The social science-based dissertation will normally include a number of standard features, including an introduction, a literature review, methodology, findings, conclusion and bibliographic references.
- You can, and should, value your own experiences and strengths as well as secondary resources.

Key questions

- How is your dissertation module organized?
- Have you received all the information about the requirements of your dissertation?
- Do you know where your strengths and weaknesses lie?

Further reading

Allison, B. and Race, P. (2004) *The Student's Guide to Preparing Dissertation and Theses*, London: RoutledgeFalmer.

Hunt, A. (2005) *Doing Your Research Project*, London: Routledge.

Todd, M., Bannister, P. and Clegg, S. (2004) 'Independent Inquiry and the Undergraduate Dissertation: Perceptions and Experiences of Final Year Social Science Students', *Assessment and Evaluation in Higher Education*, 29 (June): 335–355.

Walliman, N. S. R. (2004) *Your Undergraduate Dissertation: The Essential Guide for Success*, London: Sage.

Chapter 2

Getting support

Introduction

This chapter explores how you can get support and help with producing your dissertation. It looks specifically at the ways in which your dissertation supervisor (your institution may use a different name such as 'adviser' or 'tutor') can support you and your project and how you can make best use of the different kinds of feedback you will get from your supervisor. The chapter also considers other forms of support you could actively seek out, including that provided by staff in your library, peer and group support. By the end of this chapter, you should have a better understanding of the following:

- the role of the supervisor;
- your role in the relationship and ideas about becoming an autonomous learner;
- how to make the best use of feedback from your supervisor;
- other forms of support that may help you on your dissertation journey.

What is the role of the supervisor?

Although there are many ways to supervise a dissertation, there are some general things that can be said about the supervision process and the relationship between the student and the supervisor. This relationship is one which many institutions hold to be vital in helping students produce their dissertation:

- Supervisors offer guidance as to the best possible way of formulating and carrying out a successful project, based on their experience and aptitude for the role.

- Supervisors can provide a life line and serve as a calming influence when your dissertation appears too vast to comprehend and to undertake successfully.
- Supervisors may adopt a variety of roles throughout the dissertation process. At times they will appear to be at the centre of what you are doing, guiding and advising you.

> There is an interesting relationship between a student and a supervisor of a dissertation or research project. As such, it's going to be the first time the student experiences that they are in control – that they are the leaders of this project. I view myself in a combined role: as an inquisitor and an adviser. I always ask the student, 'What do you want to do? Where do you want to go? What are you interested in?' It is the students' answers that are important.
>
> (Dr Iain Garner (Psychology))

At other times, supervisors will be in the background, there to 'catch you' if needed; they are a resource that you can and should access as you prepare to make the leap to becoming a researcher. Try thinking of supervisors as being like the mirrors in your car: it is worth consulting them before performing any major manoeuvres! Our research (Todd *et al.* 2004, 2006) shows that students experience different types of supervision and help in the early stages of their dissertations. Students talk about the value of:

- discussing general ideas in the early meetings with their supervisor;
- helping to make the dissertation more manageable and realistic in its remit;
- help with sharpening the focus;
- help with devising a concise question;
- pointing out what should be avoided.

> Reading a bit around the topic and keeping a journal/research diary helped. Any areas that confused me were posed as questions for my supervisor.

How can my supervisor help me to identify and define my research question?

It is often the case that when supervisors first meet their students, they are presented with ambitious proposals and ideas for dissertations that resemble the kind of work expected at postgraduate level which are not feasible at undergraduate level. They would require the kind of time commitment most students don't have. One of the first things, therefore, that a dissertation supervisor will want to do is work with you to establish the limits for your work. Once these limits have been identified, the process of planning and producing a dissertation becomes far less daunting.

It is not the supervisor's responsibility to provide the student with a question but to listen to what the student has to say and to help the student to devise a suitable question. Supervisors will clearly be influenced by their own experience and expertise, but you can and should expect your supervisor to listen to your ideas and to suggest some ways to make it possible for you to fulfil your aims. Supervisors will often be helpful in providing guidance on sources. Students have noted that the following are particularly useful:

- reading lists with specific references;
- feedback on the suitability of references they have found;
- reference to general texts that can serve as a starting point.

Your supervisor can have a particularly important role in the early stages of your dissertation, when you start to formulate your ideas and look for some guidance on the possible shape and form of your dissertation. Rudestam and Newton (2001) suggest that the challenge of selecting a dissertation topic is invariably made simpler in most academic institutions with the help of a supervisor who has knowledge of the student's area of interest and who can help to narrow the focus of the dissertation.

Different dissertation supervisors and, indeed, many students have different favoured styles. I would certainly favour a style of close supervision, particularly in the early stages and ensuring that the student understands the timetable she/he is working to and then we have regular supervisions in the same day, at the same time and also ensure that the student produces this work in advance of these supervisions. So, for example, I would suggest that the students email me outlines, chapters, relevant articles, so that I can actually have a look at them before the supervision meeting.

(Alan McGauley [Social Policy])

If you are struggling to come up with proposals for your dissertation or are finding the process overwhelming, making an appointment with your tutor or supervisor allows you to outline your position and to ask for some advice (Walliman 2004). As most undergraduate students will have had little experience of formulating their own research questions up to this point, supervisors can help determine the scope of the dissertation and make it more manageable. It is important that the questions are answerable. A poorly formulated question can result in the researcher spending unnecessary time struggling to find an answer to something that cannot be answered.

Be upfront and honest about your intentions and aims. To unlock the higher grades you'll need to be keen and really dig in. Your supervisor will only be too happy to help.

What else can I expect from my supervisor?

On a more practical level, students can utilize supervisor support in order to discuss and fully understand the main assessment requirements of the dissertation in terms of:

- what the title of the dissertation is and whether it matches what you have actually done;
- its presentation (how it looks);
- organization (chapters, headed sections);
- length (not too long or too short);
- list of contents (for navigation);
- use of abstract (to summarize the dissertation);
- reference list (to demonstrate background reading).

(Walliman 2004; Todd *et al.* 2004)

Walliman (2004) stresses the importance of knowing and understanding the requirements of the dissertation and what examiners will be looking for when they allocate marks, particularly if students wish to receive the best possible grade. When the subject and title of the dissertation is agreed upon, students will be free to look towards gaining an understanding of the next steps in the dissertation process.

Make regular appointments to see your supervisor. Bear in mind the limited number of student–supervisor meetings, and make these particularly valuable.

As we have said, dissertation supervision can take very different forms according to the supervisor's choice of approach. This generally relates to whether supervisors insist on regular meetings with their students or operate on a more informal basis that allows students to ask for support when they consider it necessary. However, the majority of students sampled in our research (Todd *et al.* 2004) had, throughout the course of their dissertation, engaged in some kind of formal arrangement with their supervisor. The majority of these students saw the benefits in this, particularly the help they received in setting tasks and deadlines that served to provide additional motivation for students and the implementation of a structure throughout the dissertation process that allowed students to manage their workload more effectively.

See your dissertation supervisor as soon as you have been assigned one and when you have a basic understanding of what you want your dissertation content to be about. Set yourself a timeline and targets to organize the workload and to aid consistent progress and motivation. Always make sure prior to seeing your supervisor that you have completed what you stated you would before the meeting. It helps to think about what you want the layout of the meeting to be.

Reaching agreement with your supervisor

It is important that you and the supervisor are clear about each others' roles in this process. When researching and writing up your dissertation within higher education, it is expected that you will be operating as an autonomous learner. This means that you:

- take increasing responsibility for your own learning;
- will plan a work schedule for yourself and manage your time effectively, using interim deadlines as appropriate;
- devise your own research question(s);
- employ the research skills you have developed during your degree studies to date;
- negotiate and agree your work plan with your dissertation supervisor;
- pursue your work with the zeal and enthusiasm of a person who is thinking their way through the issues and problems that they consider to be important.

It is also important that you agree with your supervisor what the appropriate type of support is. Dissertations will certainly vary in complexity. The more complex methodology you seek to employ, the more guidance you will need. In general, a dissertation that seeks to analyse a range of theoretical sources will be easier to organize than one which relies upon drafting questionnaires, running focus groups and arranging a series of interviews. Walliman (2004) suggests that students should:

- be sure to ask what arrangements are in place for meetings with their supervisor (e.g. whether these are organized on a weekly basis or particular slots booked in advance);
- recognize that dissertation supervisors expect that when students do attend meetings they do so with something to discuss, whether these are simply ideas or written work;
- be punctual for pre-arranged meetings. This is a common courtesy;
- make sure to notify supervisors if they cannot make pre-arranged meetings;
- reach an agreement on the organization of meetings and the form these meetings take – if students find that the method used does not suit their learning style, they need to address this as early as possible and renegotiate the form that their supervision meetings take.

If you disagree with something your supervisor has suggested, let them know, and you can come to more informed outcomes.

Group supervision

There are a number of other ways in which supervision takes place. As we have said, the most common is a series of one-to-one meetings with your supervisor. These meetings could be dedicated to discussing the direction of your work or to giving feedback on the work you have already completed. But this is not the only way of accessing supervision. It is sometimes useful to have supervision meetings in groups. This allows the supervisor to provide some general advice on a range of issues, particularly at the early stages, and there is something to be said for witnessing and responding to the problems raised by other people's work.

What you will probably find is that supervisors will like to use a variety of methods; depending upon the stage you have reached in your work and the perceived benefits of intensive one-to-one meetings.

Email support

Supervisors might also suggest that you use email. This can be particularly useful when you want to address specific questions. However, be aware that email can become torrential for some academic staff, and students need to realize that supervisors have other responsibilities as well as personal lives!

Email is particularly useful to ask specific questions about references or methodology. Email can be used to send your draft chapters to your supervisor and to deal with smaller issues between supervision sessions. At times, this method can be used extensively. It is clear that emails can be used quite effectively for immediate response to issues. This avoids the problem of having to wait for a meeting, and it is often the case that specific information is easy to communicate by email. There are, however, limitations to using this method. If you want to discuss ideas and work towards a solution, it is often better to arrange to see your supervisor.

Seeking feedback on draft chapters

An important part of the supervision process consists of the feedback you receive from your supervisor. The approach to feedback will vary between institutions, but it is often the case that supervisors will provide at least some feedback on the work you produce. On completing the first draft of the dissertation proposal (or any other of the dissertation chapters), it is advised that you allow your supervisor to view your work and give his or her comments. This should help you see your work in a wider perspective. While you should take the comments of your supervisor on board – and the prospect you may have to change your work as a result – Walliman (2004) suggests that it is important to think through such alterations and their implications before doing so.

But remember, what supervisors provide as feedback is meant for guidance only. Your supervisor will advise you to do certain things to make your work clearer or to elevate its analytical features. You might feel that this advice is unwarranted. If so, as long as you are willing to take responsibility for the decision, you are free to disregard what your supervisor has to say.

We would recommend you take full advantage of all the supervision time available to you. Even if you think you have made very little progress between meetings, that contact with someone and the opportunity for discussion is invaluable. It's entirely possible that your best ideas might only make themselves apparent to you when you try and explain your thoughts to someone else, and obviously your supervisor's experience as a researcher puts him or her in the best possible place to support you.

Remember also that your dissertation is unique and supervisors are simply giving you the best advice that they can based upon their own experience and their own academic expertise. It is worth paying particular attention, however, to advice on structural issues. Such advice is often of value regardless of the subject matter of your dissertation. It is worth noting that a dissertation that ignores academic conventions and does not make sense to your supervisor is unlikely to attract a high mark.

As your knowledge of your chosen dissertation topic is not supposed to be absolute – hence one of the main reasons for doing a dissertation – supervisors will be able to tell you whether you have missed any important theories or theorists from the review of literature (Walliman 2004: 72). Supervisors can also help with practical issues such as the writing style adopted in the dissertation (formal or informal) and the required length of not only the overall dissertation but also each of the individual chapters so that the dissertation achieves a balance (Walliman 2004: 227, 231).

Students are rarely interested in having a method prescribed for them and seem far more interested in receiving feedback on their own ideas.

> We discussed methods and [my supervisor] steered me towards a much more suitable dual method.

Students also place a high value upon the advice they receive on structuring their work. The following methods seem particularly useful:

- Provision of published sources on structuring dissertations.
- Feedback on the ideas held by the students.
- Examples of dissertations on similar themes.
- Advice on the possible breakdown of each chapter.

> In the last meeting he helped to sort out a plan including word counts, sub-headings, what to include, etc.

Feedback offered by supervisors on draft versions of work is particularly valuable in providing clarity and direction to the project. Similarly, supervisors' knowledge of the subject and ability to direct students to relevant references is seen as especially helpful, as is their ability to encourage students to think differently – and more creatively – about the subject matter.

It's important to develop a relationship in which you feel comfortable with engaging in an ongoing critical dialogue related to your work so that you recognize that comments and ideas are concerned with how the academic core can be strengthened.

You will find that supervisors have a vested interest in bringing out the best in your work. They will have to read and evaluate your work and often will have to argue its merits with a second marker and even with external examiners. The clearer you can make it, the better it will be received by all concerned.

> He used a whiteboard to map out the structure of the dissertation. As I am a quite visual learner this was extremely useful for me to see it laid out.

Students claim that they prefer a combination of written and verbal feedback. Written feedback on drafts is useful to provide detailed responses to your work, though this is often made more real and useful if accompanied by a discussion between the student and the supervisor. Written feedback can sometimes appear a little blunt and critical, and this feedback can often appear more constructive if it is explained in a one-to-one meeting between the student and the supervisor. Students have said that they expect the following from the feedback they receive: 'positive comments, criticisms, areas for improvement and a rough grade' (Emma) and 'written so that amendments can be made correctly; verbal is difficult to remember' (Carrie) (Todd et al. 2004).

> An objective viewpoint on my work and suggested ways of improving it.

Why is supervision so important? Can't I just get on with my dissertation by myself?

From what has been said already, it should be clearer that the supervision process is an important part of researching and writing your dissertation. While some students will not take advantage of the supervision offered by their institutions, evidence from our research (Todd et al. 2004) would suggest that students who choose to pursue their dissertation without consulting their supervisor often find it difficult to maintain momentum and are apt to make fundamental errors in the way they approach their work. Many students, however, recognize that their supervisors have an important role to play and value their encouragement, guidance and reassurance that they are proceeding in the right direction, without taking control of their dissertations and telling them what to do.

> I want knowledge on where to go next, answers to questions I might have, possibly calming down if I'm getting stressed about having difficulty seeing 'the light at the end of the tunnel'.

Good supervisors should:

- set clear boundaries and expectations at the beginning of the supervision process;
- inform you of their availability;
- be honest about their own research strengths and limitations;
- listen;
- help you reflect on what you are doing and why;
- work in partnership with you;
- provide strategies to enable you to solve your own problems;
- ask questions, not tell you what to do, and expect you to have questions for them;
- not impose their ideas on you;
- share their own research experiences in a way that illuminates issues for you;
- challenge you to succeed.

(Kandlbinder and Peseta 2006)

Managing difficulties with supervisors

It is important that you find ways to negotiate your learning with your supervisor. Robson (2007) points out that supervisors will have their own preconceptions about what constitutes a successful project. While it is natural for students to follow the advice given, different approaches should not be ruled out if students can put forward a suitable argument for doing so and a good supervisor should be receptive to these. If you have serious concerns about the level and type of support you are receiving, Robson (2007) suggests that there should be avenues for redressing this problem. However, he (2007) also urges students to be reasonable and to acknowledge that supervisors have busy schedules. You are, therefore, advised to play your part and ensure your attendance and involvement in the process. You need to be clear of your own role within the dissertation process. At the end of the day, it remains the case that the dissertation is the responsibility of the student. Although supervisors can provide guidance, it is not their responsibility to write the dissertation for their students.

Once you are allocated to a supervisor by your university, it is not normally possible to change this arrangement. On rare occasions, however, you may find that you cannot work with the allocated supervisor. In the first instance, you should try to discuss the difficulties with the supervisor and attempt to resolve these through some agreed action plan. If you do not find it easy to do this face to face, write down your concerns in an email; this allows you to be clear about the issues (perhaps ask a friend to read it before sending it to check the tone and that the meaning is clear). If, after this, it becomes evident that the relationship has broken down irrevocably, you should contact the dissertation tutor, or whoever is responsible for the module, directly to discuss other possible arrangements. It is important to sort out such difficulties as soon as possible.

Who else may be able to help me?

Producing a dissertation can be an isolating task, one in which you find the nature of the work and study timetable reduces opportunities for mixing with other students. You may be someone who is comfortable working alone, or you may be the type of learner who is motivated and energized by a more social learning environment. In this section, we consider other people who may be able to help you successfully navigate your way through the dissertation journey and who may also be able to reduce a sense of isolation if you are experiencing this. In the previous section on changing supervisors we gave you a modest example of how you might ask a friend for support. You may wish to think about who else may have expertise or qualities that you could draw support from. Figure 2.1 (adapted from Waldman 1999) gives you an example of doing this.

Your list might include some of the following.

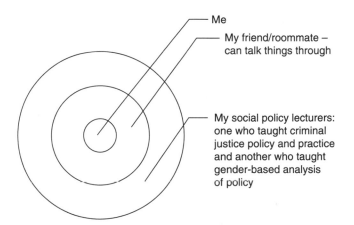

Figure 2.1 People who can help you.

Library and other institutional support services

Library staff have a wealth of expertise in research approaches and can direct you to useful databases and reference material. In many institutions, the library staff will offer specific workshops or one-to-one support for students undertaking dissertation research.

Provision of a range of written and in-person support has been a positive consequence of the expansion of higher education and growth in student numbers. Most institutions now provide comprehensive guidance on a wide range of study-skills support. These may be available through libraries or other central support units or within faculties and departments. At the start of your dissertation, you may find it helpful to access and read relevant guidance on, for example:

- writing styles;
- referencing;
- searching;
- time management.

You may have been given such documents at the start of your programme and they are now buried at the bottom of a pile of papers. Now is the time to dig them out and use them. In addition to investing in provision of written support materials, there are usually individual staff with a remit to help with specific areas of student support, particularly those with specific learning needs associated with, for example, dyslexia or having a first language other than the one they are learning in.

Other academic staff

It is common for supervisors to be assigned students who choose a topic that is not within their area of specialism. This does not have to impact on the quality of support you receive, but you might wish to consult with other academic staff in your department or other institutions for ideas on your topic, for example, with key reading. This is reasonable, but be aware that they may be very busy so do not feel offended if they are not able to respond to you within your preferred timescales. If you do want to ask something, keep your request short, simple and reasonable.

Administrative staff

Administrative staff are the backbone in institutions and will often be the best people to consult if you have practical questions about deadline, requirements for binding, etc. If you have questions that you think they could answer then try them before your supervisor: the response may be quicker.

Other students

Dissertation-writing groups are often developed to support graduate students with writing their dissertations (e.g. see www.temple.edu/writingctr/dissertationwriting) but they are also useful for undergraduate studies. Such groups might meet regularly but are informal in nature. Your university or college may have a procedure for the establishment of such groups or you could set an informal group up yourself. For them to work successfully it is important that group rules and expectations are established and maintained. Such groups could operate in a face-to-face or virtual environment and operate as a form of action-learning set (McGill and Brockbank 2004). The benefits may include:

- reducing isolation;
- motivation to stick to project timelines;
- critical friends with whom to discuss specific ideas, challenges and 'knotty problems';
- sounding issues out in advance of meeting a supervisor;
- putting things in perspective if you are feeling stressed or under pressure;
- sharing resources and search results.

Such benefits can be gained through one-to-one peer or pair support with like-minded fellow students(s). Through online tools such as *del.icio.us* you have many opportunities to share resources such as citations.

Work-based supervisors, colleagues and users of services

If you are working and studying or on a course such as social work, involving access to a work environment that is related to your subject of study, and many social science students will be as part of a placement, internship, through voluntary or paid work, you may be able to discuss ideas and seek guidance or feedback from supervisors and colleagues there. If you are undertaking an applied or practice-focused dissertation, this will be invaluable. You may also wish to consult with staff from other agencies who you have identified as being particularly experienced or expert in an area related to your topic.

Online support

In addition to your institutional virtual learning environment, there are many online social networking sites, information and discussion groups where you may find access to help and information from others in your discipline area. For the social sciences, see www.socialpsychology.org/forums/student and see www.thestudentroom.co.uk for all subject interests.

Friends and family

There are all sorts of ways in which friends and family may provide emotional and practical support – from making you cups of coffee to reading and proof-reading extracts of content. We all want to achieve a good study/home/work to life balance, and each of us has our own way of finding our way through this, but we recognize this is not easy!

Key messages

- Initially, ask your supervisor for advice on your choice of topic and your reading.
- Talk to your supervisor, preferably at regular meetings, the frequency of which should be agreed upon mutually.
- If this is allowed in your department, show draft chapters to your supervisor as soon as you have them: give your supervisor time to read, think and give feedback.
- Your supervisor will offer constructive criticisms of your work: that is why he or she is there. It is not a criticism of you, or of your ability. Do not be shy or embarrassed by this.
- Your personal supervisor is a resource: use that resource to your advantage. Ask them questions: about methodology, theory or anything else that may occur. You are not expected to be an instant expert – that's their job!
- Your supervisor will help you but not do your work for you. Supervisors can only work with what you bring them.
- Try to draw a network of other support around you to reduce any sense of isolation and to increase access to useful expertise and help – both on and off campus.

Key questions

- Are you clear about the role of your supervisor and how he or she can support you and your work?
- Are you making the most of the objectivity and honesty the supervisor can offer to help you improve your work?
- Do you prepare for meetings to make the most of the time you have available?
- Are you keeping in touch throughout the work process?
- Who else can support you with your work and how?

Further reading

Kandlbinder, P. and Peseta, T. (2006) *In Supervisors' Words: An Insider's View of Postgraduate Supervision*, Sydney: Institute for Teaching and Learning, University of Sydney.

McGill, I. and Brockbank, A. (2004) *The Action Learning Handbook: Powerful Techniques for Education*, London: Routledge.

Robson, C. (2007) *How to Do a Research Project: A Guide for Undergraduate Students*, Oxford: Blackwell.

Rudestam, K. E. and Newton, R. R. (1992) *Surviving Your Dissertation: A Comprehensive Guide to Content and Process*, London: Sage.

Todd, M., Bannister, P. and Clegg, S. (2004) 'Independent Inquiry and the Undergraduate Dissertation: Perceptions and Experiences of Final-Year Social Science Students', *Assessment and Evaluation in Higher Education*, 29 (3): 335–355.

Waldman, J. (1999) *Help Yourself to Learning at Work*, Lyme Regis: Russell House.

Walliman, N. (2004) *Your Undergraduate Dissertation: The Essential Guide for Success*, London: Sage.

Chapter 3

Getting started on your dissertation

Introduction

This chapter has been written to help you with ideas and strategies for planning your dissertation most effectively. Often the dissertation involves many months of work, and it is important that you manage your time and schedule effectively. The dissertation is usually an extended piece of work that requires good organizational and time-management skills to complete to a high standard. Unsurprisingly, because of competing demands on time, many students do not always devise and follow a structured work schedule, which can have implications for the quality of work produced, not to mention your stress levels.

By the end of this chapter, you should have a better understanding of:

- how to best prepare for your dissertation;
- how to find a dissertation topic;
- how to refine that topic into a workable research question;
- how to plan so you will manage to complete all your work before the deadline.

How to get started with preparing a dissertation

The first stage in preparing a dissertation is deciding the topic you wish to research in detail and write about. It's worth reminding yourself that the dissertation is a piece of assessment that provides you with a unique opportunity to explore in depth a subject in which you have a personal interest or to further develop an interest from previous study. It may also be that you want to choose a topic related to a career aspiration. Researching and writing a dissertation is hard work, but it should also be rewarding, because it represents individual academic achievement of a kind that may make a difference to your field of enquiry. One dissertation student was very clear about the benefits of her research: 'It's been a valuable experience for me it's so different from other [types of assessment]. With other essays you can rush them if you have to ... but this is so much work, you can't rush it. It demands more' (Todd *et al.* 2004: 340).

Some of the first stages of your dissertation are quite similar to deciding where to go on your vacation this year. There are many factors that may influence your choice: will you choose a trekking holiday in the Andes or a beach holiday on the Mediterranean? There will be other factors to take into account: What resources (funds) do you have available?, How much time do you have? and What do you enjoy doing?

Selecting a topic for your dissertation, like choosing where to go on holiday, is not always easy. Some people are fortunate: an idea for a dissertation may pop into their mind immediately; they have always been interested in an area and want to do more in-depth research into it. For many, however, this is not the case, and you may need to be more systematic in your search for *the* dissertation question or topic that you wish to explore further.

You're likely to do a great deal of thinking and background reading before you reach a final decision about the topic in which you want to invest a lot of time and effort (just as you wouldn't spend a lot of money on a foreign holiday without taking a bit of time deciding where to go). Research has shown that the dissertation supervisor is crucial in helping final-year students to find their topic – so don't be afraid to ask for advice. This dissertation student notes why her dissertation supervision was so important in defining her dissertation topic: 'I'm not sure that I could have come up with the question on my own. I didn't know what I could answer; I didn't know what it would benefit me to do' (Todd *et al.* 2004: 343).

Finding a topic for the dissertation

So, it is at this stage that you need to spend time thinking about your choice of topic. There are a number of things that you can do to stimulate thoughts about a dissertation topic.

*   Start talking to members of academic staff and other students in your department (either directly or in an online discussion forum) at an early stage about your ideas.
*   Make up a list of unresolved questions and issues you had from other courses and modules that you have studied or intend to study. You

could use the reading and knowledge from these to develop a dissertation question.

- Read newspapers and other media to identify topical issues related to areas of social policy, politics, sociology, criminology, etc.
- Draw upon your own experience (as an employee, a parent, part of a campaigning group, a student, a patient and so on) and use this experience to help you define your topic area.
- Think about a book you found interesting or scan academic journals to find areas that capture your interest and your imagination. Are there any key writers who have shaped your interest or whose views conflict with yours?

Clarifying ideas and narrowing focus

So, let's assume that you now have a number of potential topic areas in mind. In fact, you may feel you now have too much choice and don't know which area to focus upon! The following checklist may be helpful in deciding which topic to develop into your dissertation research question:

- Can the topic you have selected be addressed in an appropriately academic manner?
- Can the topic be fully explored within the time frame you have for this module (noting that you will have commitments to other modules as well as other non-academic commitments)?
- What are the resource constraints of the dissertation. For example, you may be interested in exploring the views of Scottish members of parliament on the issue of Scottish independence, but how feasible is this in terms of travel time and costs?
- Will the topic be able to sustain your interest over the months to come?

In summary, when you have identified an area that you would like to pursue further, you need to assess whether your topic can be researched in the time available and with the resources that you have. You should avoid too broad a topic or one that is overly ambitious: it is better to find a thoroughly researched and argued answer to a small question than to fail to find the answer to one which is too big or diffuse. Your main interest in the topic may be:

- an area of social life;
- a type of method that you would like to use;

- a body of theory that you are interested in exploring.

Bringing all three of these together is a way of narrowing the focus of the dissertation into a manageable project.

Always keep in mind that your dissertation is an extremely small piece of research: at every turn you should be narrowing the focus, not expanding it. A good piece of well-argued and focused research with a small scope will get a far better mark than a larger incoherent one.

Another way of narrowing the focus is to think about what you are particularly interested in. Write a paragraph that would give someone else a clear picture of the issues. How has your interest developed over time? Can you identify incidents or experiences that have generated your interest? Finally, consider where would you like the work to lead in the longer term and whether this research is connected with work you currently do or would like to do at some stage.

In the following case study, Tsang Kwok Kuen, a social science graduate, describes what he felt was important in choosing his dissertation topic.

Case study: choosing my dissertation topic

My research topic was on the theme of ingratiation. Why did I choose it? It was because I had observed that many people in Hong Kong seemed to like to flatter others. Why did they do that? I didn't know, so I really wanted to understand this phenomenon deeply. In fact, I tried to study it when I was at secondary school. I took a subject then called Liberal Studies that required me to conduct some research. I chose to study ingratiation. Because of my lack of research skills at that time, I didn't design my research very well and found out nothing. This bad result motivated me to study the same area and topic for my dissertation because I was still curious to find out more about ingratiation.

After deciding a research area, I started to read literature. I didn't only read the literature related to ingratiation but also read the Chinese Indigenized Social Psychology literature. Actually, I know that some of my friends didn't read much literature. This was because the literature was too difficult and boring for them. However, I discovered the literature was not as boring as many people thought – maybe the discussions in the literature were related to things I was really interested in. As I kept reading, I got more and more insights into my topic. These insights motivated me to read and think continually. As a result, I formed my own idea about how to write the dissertation.

My experience tells me that doing something you are interested in is very important for you when you are writing a dissertation. Therefore, your interest is an essential source for you to start to think about your own project. For example, one of my friends decided to study the relationship between pets and pet owners. It was because she loved animals and had many pets. If you can find something like this you will enjoy and be motivated to do this difficult piece of work. Look and find a topic from an area you're interested in!

(Tsang Kwok Kuen)

Having identified your topic, you must then develop a question, identifying what you hope to learn. Finding a question sounds as though it will be easier than finding a topic, but, in fact, research questions usually need to be shaped and crafted quite extensively. We will look at this issue in the next section.

What is a good research question?

It is important to start your thinking about the dissertation with a *question* once you have chosen a topic heading. The question sets out what you hope to learn about the topic. This question, together with your approach, will guide and structure the choice of data to be collected and analysed. Some research questions focus your attention onto the relationship of particular theories and concepts, for example, 'How does gender relate to career choices of members of different religions?'

Some research questions aim to open an area to let possible new theories emerge: 'What is going on here?' is the most basic research question in exploratory research. For an undergraduate dissertation, your question needs to be much more targeted than either of these.

Creating a research question is a task. Good research questions are formed, shaped and worked on and are very rarely simply found. This student describes his experiences of struggling to find a question:

I knew what I wanted to write about but I couldn't get a question to match. My original question was too vague and unanswerable. In terms of tightening it up, I knew I wanted to link disability to employment. I tried to get a question from that but it was a descriptive question that I ended up scrapping on the advice of the supervisor, he told me it wasn't any good as a research question.

(Todd *et al.* 2004: 340)

You start with what interests you (the topic area we discussed above) and refine it until it is academically rigorous and workable. There is no recipe for the perfect research question, but there are bad research questions. The following guidelines highlight some of the features of good questions:

- relevant;
- manageable in terms of research and in terms of your own academic abilities;
- substantial and with original dimensions;
- consistent with the requirements of the assessment;
- clear and simple;
- interesting.

Relevant

The question will be of academic and intellectual interest to people in your field. The question arises from issues raised in the literature or in practice. You should be able to establish a clear purpose for your research in relation to the chosen field. For example, are you filling a gap in knowledge, analysing academic assumptions or professional practice, monitoring a development in practice, comparing different approaches or testing theories within a specific population?

Manageable

You need to be realistic about the scope and scale of the project. The question you ask must be within your ability to tackle it. For example:

- Are you able to *access* people, statistics or documents from which you will collect the data you need to address the question fully?
- Are you able to relate the concepts of your research question to the observations, phenomena, indicators or variables you can access?
- Can this data be accessed within the limited *time* and *resources* you have available to you?

Sometimes a research question appears feasible, but when you start your fieldwork or library study, it proves otherwise. In this situation, it is important to write up the problems you have come across honestly and to reflect on what has been learnt. You should also develop a contingency plan to anticipate possible problems of access.

Substantial and (within reason) original

The question should not simply copy questions asked in other final-year modules or modules previously undertaken. The question you devise should show your own social science imagination and your ability to construct and develop research issues. And it needs to give sufficient scope to develop into a dissertation.

Consistent with the requirements of the assessment

The question must give you the scope to satisfy the learning outcomes of the course. For example, you can choose to conduct a theoretical study, one that does not contain analysis of empirical data. In this case, it will be necessary for you to think carefully before making such a choice. You would be required to give an account of your methodology, to explain why theoretical analysis was the most appropriate way of addressing the question and how you have gone about using theoretical models to produce new insights about the subject. Make sure that you study the requirements of the dissertation and that your research question will fulfil these requirements. Again, if you are still not sure, a discussion with your supervisor or course leader would be helpful here.

Check your home department's dissertation archive: ask in the school office to see dissertations on your topic.

Clear and simple

The complexity of a question can frequently hide unclear thoughts and lead to a confused research process. A very elaborate research question, or a question which is not differentiated into different parts, may hide concepts that are contradictory or potentially not relevant at all. Getting this clear and thought through is one of the hardest parts of your work.

Equally, you will want to get started with your literature review and data collection, and you may feel tempted to 'make do' with a broad and vague research question for the moment. However, a muddled question is likely to generate muddled data and equally muddled analysis.

If you create a clear and simple research question, you may find that it becomes more complex as you think about the situation you are studying and undertake the literature review. Having one key question with several sub-components will guide your research here.

Interesting

This is key: the question needs to be one that interests you and is likely to remain intriguing for the duration of the project. There are two traps to be avoided.

First, some questions are *convenient* – the best you can come up with when you are asked to state a question on a form, maybe – or perhaps the question fits in with your units so you decide it will suffice.

Second, some questions are *fads*. They arise out of a particular set of personal circumstances, for example, a job application. Once the circumstances change you can lose enthusiasm for the topic and it becomes very tedious.

Make sure that you have a real, grounded interest in your research question and that you can explore this and back it up by academic and intellectual debate. It is your interest that will motivate you to keep working and to produce a good dissertation.

As you develop your research question, think carefully about what you would like to find out about. You might have a hypothesis – i.e. a belief about something (founded upon evidence) – which has never been fully tested, proved or disproved. You may, on the other hand, want to couch your interest in terms of an exploration of issues, attitudes or experiences or as a question. Write a list of all the questions you want to answer and group them into priorities or hierarchies and show the connections between them. At this stage, you may want to do some weeding out of overlapping or less relevant questions. It is helpful to list your questions and then to answer why you want to know the answer and how it will help you to pursue your overall enquiry.

Taking notes

The process of thinking about the dissertation topic and question is an evolving one. It may help to get some form of personal recording of the ideas, links and resources that you come across in the initial thinking and information-gathering stages. Do not simply rely on your memory to store all the strands of information you come across. A key part of success in dissertation-writing is being organized and systematic in your approach, and the earlier you can adopt this, the better. It is found that keeping a research diary, where you could also record your thoughts, can prove particularly useful. This type of note-taking may link into the writing of other learning logs or personal development planning you are doing already within your degree. Many people find it useful to keep a research notebook in which you can record:

- questions or ideas that interest you;
- possible ways of researching these;
- references to follow up at a later stage;
- sources of information that you have found useful;
- notes on articles and papers you have read or programmes you have seen or heard.

You should keep an accurate record of the bibliographical details of all the material that you read: doing this as you go along will save an enormous amount of time at the end of the project. For more information on literature searching and managing your bibliographical resources, see Chapter 4.

Time management and work planning

Dissertations usually have a long lead-in time so it is essential that you think about the various stages of work that need to be undertaken and get into good habits early on in the process, for example, keeping records of searches undertaken, ideas that crop up and material to be sought after and incorporated.

You might want to devise a schedule of work from start to finish, or monthly plans, perhaps in discussion with your supervisor or tutor. Nearer the deadline, you may wish to use weekly schedules to keep you on track.

> Brainstorming the key research questions, concepts, themes and thoughts gave me some idea of the scale of the task ahead. A timeline was then produced to outline the main stages of development in the project.

If you are undertaking empirical work, your planning will need to be even more detailed so that you are aware of slippage that may affect completion of the research.

You will need to allow time for the following:

- refining the research question/hypothesis;
- checking if your project needs Ethics Committee/School Research Governance approval;
- designing the framework for the literature review;
- undertaking the literature search and using the framework to develop the review;
- developing the methodology for fieldwork and identifying appropriate methods;

- if required, gaining access and agreeing arrangements for data collection;
- collecting the data;
- coding or transcribing the data;
- analysing data;
- developing the discussion;
- writing up the study and conclusions.

This will all require careful management of time and keeping a check on progress. You may find it helpful to develop a chart indicating when various stages of work will be undertaken, and with what contingencies. A Gantt chart might work well here. This is a bar-chart-like representation of the work breakdown of your dissertation. It can be made using Microsoft Office Excel to design stacked bar charts. Or you might prefer to use specific project-management software. Microsoft Office Project is one such piece of software that helps you to control your work and schedule your time. Simple project-management templates can also help you. You might have come across these kinds of template as part of your personal-development planning, or you may devise your own charts and milestone indicators.

Whichever approach you adopt to help you manage your time for the dissertation, you need to be really honest with yourself about what you can do in the time that is available. Your supervisor will be able to give you guidance on whether your plans are realistic.

Key messages

- Ideas for topics can come from a variety of sources: staff, other students, past modules and essays, the media or the internet.
- Choose a topic that will sustain your interest over the coming year and one that has some background and existing literature to it.
- Your research questions should be relevant, manageable, substantial, consistent with your assessment, clear and interesting.
- Write things down as they happen, from your initial ideas to problems and your own feelings about the project.
- Consider project-management organizational tools that may help you.

Key questions

- What specific topic are you really interested in?
- Have you tried formulating questions in different ways?

- Will your question result in work that will fulfil the requirements of your dissertation?
- Are you keeping notes of what you read and your ideas? Is your note-taking time efficient? Are the notes useful to you?
- Have you mapped out the work that you need to do from start to finish for your dissertation?

Further reading

Bryman, A. (2008) *Social Research Methods*, 3rd edn, Oxford: Oxford University Press.

Creswell, J. W. (2003) *Research Design: Qualitative, Quantitative and Mixed Method Approaches*, London: Sage.

Punch, K. F. (2005) *Introduction to Social Research: Quantitative and Qualitative Approaches*, London: Sage.

Seale, C. (2006) *Researching Society and Culture*, London: Sage.

Chapter 4

Literature searching

Introduction

Having completed essays and projects throughout your course, you will be familiar with techniques to locate relevant information. However, you may find that you need to 'step up a gear' for your project or dissertation. This chapter offers a reminder of search techniques and places to search to find literature for your dissertation. It does not deal with finding data; this will be covered in Chapter 6. By the end of this chapter, you will have a better understanding of:

- search strategies;
- where to search;
- how to access the resources you find;
- what to do when you find the resources;
- who to ask for help.

Why search the literature?

Conducting a systematic and thorough literature search will ensure that you find all the resources that will help you to throw light on the questions you are researching. A literature search will show you whether someone has already answered the questions you are asking, or it will show you how other researchers have approached similar problems.

It is worth remembering that literature is more than just books; literature includes all of the following:

- books (reference, text, monographs);
- conference proceedings;
- encyclopaedias;
- journal articles;

- magazine articles;
- newspapers;
- official publications;
- online material;
- patents;
- published DVD/video material;
- reports;
- standards;
- theses;
- TV/radio broadcasts.

There is a wealth of information out there. It is, therefore, really important to have good search strategies and evaluation methods in place to make sure you find the most relevant literature for your study.

Working out search strategies

You probably started to scan the literature as you were in the process of choosing your research topic. The purpose of this initial scan is to map your topic area to get a sense of what has been done before, where the gaps are and to help you focus your topic and identify your research questions.

In order to come up with your search strategies, you can use a process involving brainstorming and concept mapping. The process suggested below is adapted from Tysick (2004).

Brainstorming

In this phase, you note down all the ideas you have about the topic you want to research. At this stage, you just write down everything that you can think of. You need to ask yourself questions about your topic based on your brainstorm:

- Is the topic too big or too small?
- Are there any connections?
- What do you already know about the things you have noted down?
- Where will your research fit into this picture?

Figure 4.1 shows the beginning of a brainstorm on anti-social behaviour.

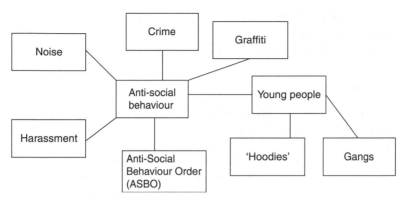

Figure 4.1 Anti-social behaviour brainstorm.

Concept mapping

In answering your questions, a set of concepts and variables will emerge. These can be organized hierarchically and linked with phrases. In Figure 4.2, the concepts are in bold, and the linkage phrases in smaller plain text.

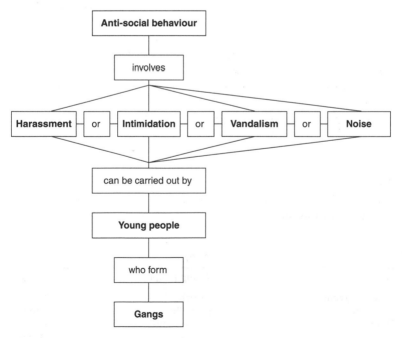

Figure 4.2 Anti-social behaviour concept map.

Organization in this way allows you to identify the most important concepts, as it will not be possible to search for all concepts in your literature search. These maps can then be the focus of your search strategy.

Search terms

Look at the main concepts in your concept map and then come up with synonyms for each one of them. You might find using a thesaurus or encyclopaedia useful for this. It is important to have a list of synonyms because most search tools will only search for the terms that you use. This means that you could potentially miss out on a lot of useful information in other records. Table 4.1 shows examples of synonyms for anti-social behaviour terms.

The components can then be combined into search statements using Boolean operators. You should aim to produce a series of search statements.

The power of little words

You would never have thought that the Boolean operators AND, NOT and OR could be so powerful. But as soon as you realize their power, you will be using them all the time. Instead of having to trawl through hundreds of references on 'binge drinking', you can introduce other concepts into the topic such as 'students' and 'social class' to make it much more specific and to produce a far more manageable list of references at the stroke of a key.

Here is an overview of some common operators.

AND

When you use this operator, the search will only return items which contain both terms in your search. Using AND can help to reduce the number of returns and to make them more specific. In Figure 4.3, the

Table 4.1 Anti-social behaviour synonyms

Vandalism	Young people	Gang
Destructiveness	Youth	Group
Violence	Juvenile	Ring
Damage	Adolescent	Mob
Harm	Teenager	Band

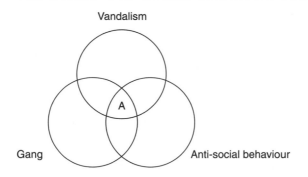

Vandalism

A

Gang

Anti-social behaviour

A = Gang AND Anti-social behaviour AND Vandalism

Figure 4.3 The AND function.

following search term was entered: 'Anti-social behaviour AND vandalism AND gang.' Only sources that include the three search terms – anti-social behaviour, vandalism and gang – will be returned.

NOT

When you use this operator, the search will remove the references that come after the NOT. Like AND, NOT can reduce the number of references returned, thus making the search more focused. In Figure 4.4, the following search term was entered: 'Anti-social behaviour NOT harassment.' This search will not return sources that mention both harassment and anti-social behaviour, but will return any others that mention anti-social behaviour.

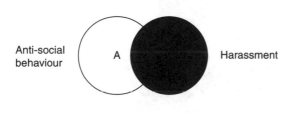

Anti-social
behaviour

A

Harassment

A = Anti-social behaviour NOT Harassment

Figure 4.4 The NOT function.

OR

If you are looking to have a broader search, the OR will be the operator you use first. Here, your search will return all the terms in your search. In an OR statement, your terms should be synonyms for each other. In Figure 4.5, the following search term was entered: 'Vandalism OR damage OR destructiveness.' This search will return any sources that contain any one of the search terms (vandalism, damage or destructiveness).

You can also use the Boolean operators together:

- Anti-social behaviour AND (vandalism OR damage)
- Anti-social behaviour NOT (harassment OR noise)

In more complex searches, such as these, the brackets enclose the search terms. So, the first search will return any sources that include the term 'anti-social behaviour' and either 'vandalism' or 'damage'. In the second search, sources containing 'anti-social behaviour' but neither the words 'harassment' nor 'noise' will be returned.

There are other devices you can use in your search. For example, you can limit references identified by dates, language, peer review and full text availability. You can use quotation marks to search for exact phrases. There are a range of wildcards that you can use. An asterisk (*) is used to search for words from the same root. A search for *vandal** would return 'vandal', 'vandals', 'vandalism', 'vandalize' (or 'vandalise'), 'vandalizes', 'vandalized', etc. A question mark (?) would help you search for variations in spelling. A search for *organi?ation* would return both 'organization' and 'organisation'.

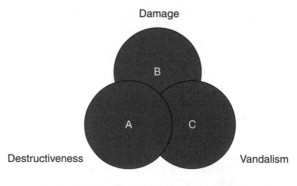

A+B+C = Damage OR Destructiveness OR Vandalism

Figure 4.5 The OR function.

Not all search engines use Boolean searching or wildcards. Therefore, it is worth using the help options in order to get the best advice for using the individual search tools.

The success of your search depends on you taking time to think about the concepts in your search strategy and employing the right commands to link those concepts together.

Starting searching

With your search statements in place, it is time to start your search. Hart (1998: 35) suggests a three-phase approach to identifying relevant items for your research study:

1 published books;
2 journal articles;
3 theses and conference papers.

You begin by searching for published books. Skim them for relevance, check their bibliographies for useful items and add them to your list. Then search for journal articles. Again, look at the reference list and add any that look interesting to your own. Repeat the same process with theses and conference papers. As you see, this is an iterative process. You keep collecting relevant items and growing your bibliographical list.

Below are some suggestions as to where you can start your search for the three types of literature highlighted above. It is worth going to see your subject librarian as they will be able to point you to the best catalogues, databases and indexes for your topic that are available at your institution.

Published books

Your library catalogue is a good place to start your search for published books. However, you might want to extend this out to search the catalogues of the following:

- The Library of Congress: the largest library in the world, based in the USA.
- The European Library: this catalogue offers access to the resources of 47 national libraries in Europe.
- The British Library: the biggest library in the UK, which receives a copy of everything published in the UK.

- COPAC: the merged catalogues of major UK universities and national libraries.
- OPACS: library networked catalogues in education, research and public sectors.

Journal articles

In order to search for journal articles, you need to use databases, abstracts and indexes. Here are some that you might look at:

- Web of Knowledge: this is a research platform that will find a range of documents: journal articles, conference proceedings and websites.
- International Bibliography of the Social Sciences: this bibliography is focused on the social sciences. It covers journal articles, books, reviews and chapters from edited books.
- Applied Social Science Index and Abstracts (ASSIA): this has records from over 500 different journals.
- Sociological Abstracts: this abstracts and indexes international literature on sociology and related disciplines.

Other than using one's university library and searching by subject, bibliographic databases are great search engines when looking for online journals.

Theses and conference papers

Abstracts and indexes can also be used to find these kinds of literature. But there are some more specific sites:

- Proquest Dissertation and Theses Database: the world's most comprehensive collection of dissertations and theses, containing more than 2.4 million entries.
- Index to Theses in Great Britain and Ireland: this lists the theses accepted for higher degrees in Great Britain and Ireland since 1716.

Online gateways

There are also other places where you can start your search. Here are some online gateways:

- BUBL: catalogues internet sources, using the same system of categorization you see in the library (http://bubl.ac.uk).

- Intute: provides access to web resources for the social sciences and has the benefit of being evaluated and selected by subject specialists (www.intute.ac.uk).
- Sociosite: links to the best sociological sites on the web (www.sociosite.net).
- SocioWeb: a guide to sociological resources on the internet (www.socioweb.com).

Your subject librarian will be able to give you more information about these information portals and will be able to demonstrate their use. Do visit your library and use the support of the staff there.

The literature search was probably my least favourite task, but library catalogues and tools such as EBSCO [online full-text database, http://search.ebscohost.com] helped. After reading initial articles, using their reference lists to locate further readings, and following up recommendations made by my dissertation supervisor also helped.

Search engines

Search engines are programs that can search documents on the internet for keywords and then list those documents where the keywords were found. Well-known search engines include: Yahoo, Windows Live Search, Ask.com and Google.

Google Scholar, however, focuses specifically on academic literature including peer-reviewed journal articles, theses, books, preliminary works, abstracts and technical reports. Many university library systems are linked to Google Scholar. If your library subscribes to the journal, you may be directed to the text via a library link after the title of the result, but if it does not, you may find you cannot access full articles without payment. It is advisable to use Google Scholar's advanced search option, which allows you to search more precisely, for example, by exact phrase, author or publication and by date. Google Scholar is only one of a number of search engines and citation databases. As with other sources, it does not offer complete coverage of scholarly works. If you are looking for citation results, look at other sources as well such as Web of Knowledge. Other sources will use different searching options, some of which will allow greater refinement of your searches.

The bliss of browsing

The previous section has focused particularly on online searches (from catalogues to information gateways). However, you should not underestimate how productive perusing your library collection can be. It is worth spending some time browsing the shelves in the library. Once you have located a book that your search has highlighted, have a look and see what's placed around it – you never know what you might find.

Sourcing references

Having searched a number of sources, you might be overwhelmed by the volume of literature that your search produces. This is why it is so important to have defined the parameters of your topic when you begin planning your research, so that you can ascertain what is relevant to your topic and what is not. You should remember, however, that your dissertation is more than the literature that you review; so, set yourself a timeframe for searching and stop when your time is up. You must ensure that you leave sufficient time to cover the rest of your research.

With a list of references that you want to look at, you need to source those documents. If you are lucky, the document will be available at your own library. In this case, you will need only to go and collect it. Increasingly, universities have a large number of resources available in electronic form. In order to access these, you may well need a special login code, for example, 'Athens' authentication (Athens is an Access Management System developed by Eduserv that simplifies access to the electronic resources your organization has subscribed to. Eduserv is a not-for-profit, professional IT services group (www.athensams.net/)) but once you have logged in, you will be able to download and print the source you are interested in. Check with your librarian how you can access the online resources. Sometimes, however, your library will not have a copy of the reference that you need. Initially, it is worth asking your supervisor if they have a copy you could borrow; if it is a key text in your area, they might well do. If not, then you need to see where the copies are held. If another library in your city has a copy, you might decide to go and access the document there. Most libraries have 'reading access' rights, meaning that you can go to their library and read the source but not take it away. You are unlikely, however, to get access to their electronic services. It is best to phone ahead and see whether it is worth you making the trip.

If you are struggling to find a resource, your university will most likely operate an Inter Library Loan (ILL) system. This means that the source you need will be ordered from another library and delivered to you. If the source is a book, you will be given a date by which you will need to return it. If it is a journal article, then you will probably be sent a photocopy by post or, increasingly, by email. You may have to pay for this service – so make sure that the source is relevant for your research.

At this stage, you will have access to the sources that will be the foundation to your research. It is worth checking your list with your supervisor; they will be able to tell you whether there are key references missing.

Working with sources

As you collect your list of references, you can keep a check on their relevance without initially reading them all in depth. You can pick up clues as to whether your source will be useful by reading the abstract, the conclusion and/or the contents page.

You will also need to evaluate the documents you have retrieved. Ask questions about the author of the work you are accessing, his or her academic qualifications, the work he or she has done before, and the institution where the work was carried out (Gash 2000: 101). If you are working with internet sources, you need to be even more careful when evaluating what you read because anyone can put anything on the internet. Ask the same questions as above but also consider the accuracy of the information, any indications of authorship, dates when the site was last updated and how you accessed the site (Was there a link from another site?). The Purdue University Online Writing Lab (http://owl.english.purdue.edu/), the Open University's SAFARI (www.open.ac.uk/safari/index.php), and Intute's Virtual Training Suite (www.vts.intute.ac.uk) are all useful sources on evaluating both print and online sources. You will probably also find that your library offers an information literacy tutorial which will guide you in how to evaluate your sources.

At this stage, you should disregard texts that do not meet the criteria of your study. Conversely, look at the bibliographies again and check whether there are sources listed there that look interesting but which are not on your developing reference list.

It is really important that you keep a hold of all the bibliographic details of the sources that you have collected. There is nothing more frustrating than spending time that you do not have searching for the details of a source. As you collect your sources, you should be keeping a note of:

- author;
- title (of article, journal, chapter, book);

- editor (for edited books);
- edition, volume, issue;
- publisher;
- place of publication;
- web page and date of access for internet sources;
- key words;
- how you found the source – keep a record in your search strategies (some information databases will allow you to save searches and set up alerts).

You might also want to add in your comments on the source, to remind you at a later date why this particular piece was important.

There are different ways that you can store this information. The least technical is to make a note of details on index cards, which you then store alphabetically in an index-card box. You could, instead, keep a record in a Word or Excel document. The sorting function will enable you to quickly and easily arrange the references into alphabetical order; the find function will allow you to search for specific pieces of information. Alternatively, you might decide to use a piece of bibliographic software, such as Endnote or Refworks. These tools help you to manage your references by creating a database which can be searched and organized. They will keep all of your references in one place, they sometimes link to databases such as Web of Knowledge (www.isiwebofknowledge.com/), and they will make constructing consistent reference lists much easier. It is likely that your institution will support one of these tools. So, go to the library, find out which one is available and sign up for some training. If you start to use the bibliographic software early in your dissertation process, you will find that it saves you time in the long run.

Whichever system you use, however, you should aim to keep complete and systematic notes on your references.

Reading the references

You should now have a list of and access to references which are relevant for your study. Now you should start reading those sources critically. Look for the key themes in the documents and try and identify how the sources fit together.

This process is going to be time-consuming because you will be reading a large amount of material. Furthermore, once you start your reading, you might find that some of the literature is of little relevance to your study. Don't panic, this is something that many researchers and dissertation students go through and is often a necessary part of the process. It is better to read something that is not central to your dissertation than miss something that might be an important and relevant contribution to the field.

While reading, make notes about the central themes and arguments of the book, chapter or article. Try and get a sense of the theoretical perspective of the author; this will be of use when you come to organize and present your literature review. Also, emphasize the way in which the piece of literature you are reading seeks to set itself apart from other literature. Importantly, start to think critically about the piece you are reading: Ask what this person is trying to say and why? How is it different from the way others have dealt with this issue? This critical component is very important as it demonstrates that you are engaging with relevant literature in an appropriate manner and that you can discriminate between different perspectives and approaches that exist within your chosen field.

Keep track of what you read and try to organize all your notes into themes, for example: How does what I am taking notes from fit into my research focus?

As you read, ensure that you also keep a note of page numbers. This is important if you want to come back to the source to check your interpretation and also, when you write your dissertation, you will need to include page numbers in your citations. Making a note now can stop you wasting a lot of time later trying to find an elusive quote. Good note-taking and critical reading in the initial stages of your dissertation will lead to a much more effective and focused literature review.

Moving to the literature review

The literature review incorporates the notes that you have made during the reading of the literature that you have found. It is an important part of your dissertation because it performs a number of related functions. It demonstrates to your reader that you have read widely and that you are aware of the range of debates that have taken place within the given field. It provides the proof that you have more than a good grasp of the breadth and depth of the topic of the dissertation.

The literature review can provide the rationale for the research question in the study. This can be done by highlighting specific gaps in the literature – questions that have not been answered (or even asked) and areas of research that have not been conducted within your chosen field. In this way, the literature review can provide a justification of your own research.

It can allow you to build on work that has already been conducted. For example, you might adopt a similar methodological or theoretical approach in your work to one that exists within the literature yet place your actual emphasis elsewhere. In this way, you are building on work that has already been conducted by adopting similar strategies and concepts yet focusing the question on something that interests you.

It also helps to define the broad context of your study, placing your work within a well-defined academic tradition. Poor dissertations often fail to relate to broader debates within the academic community. They may have a well-defined research question, yet, without placing this question in the appropriate context, the research can lose its significance. The literature review, therefore, can add weight to your question by framing it within broader debates within the academic community.

Drawing on support from others

Library staff

Library staff are available to answer general enquiries in person, by telephone and online (by email or online form). For subject-specific enquiries, subject librarians or subject specialists will usually be the best people to help, including advice regarding special collections. To get the most out of your subject librarian, make sure you are prepared before you make contact. You may need to make an appointment to discuss your queries.

- Think about your questions and write them down in advance.
- If you have a query about a specific publication or research report, allow enough time for the material to be located – an inter-library loan may be required.
- It will help the librarian if you give detailed information about your topic and mention which information sources you have already consulted.

If you have queries about searches, think of key words and terms to start with. The librarian may have ideas on other helpful search terms.

How can a librarian help with choosing a topic?

The librarian can help you to identify relevant bibliographical databases to search in order to identify appropriate materials. The librarian can then help with:

- explaining the search strategy;
- identifying keywords;

- navigating an information database;
- how to save searches and results;
- how to access full-text links;
- how to set up alerts;
- how to broaden or focus your search;
- explaining about subject terms and descriptors;
- explaining about the thesaurus for getting the best results from any bibliographical tool;
- citation searching.

Libraries have online and paper-based guidance on a wide range of information issues. Typically, these include:

- searching databases and finding research literature;
- web searching;
- how to reference (including citing electronic resources) and managing references (for example, using software);
- new developments in search tools and websites;
- academic skills such as writing effectively;
- online tutorials (for example, to use the International Bibliography of Social Sciences (IBSS) (www.lse.ac.uk/collections/IBSS/) or Web of Knowledge successfully);
- advice and help for students with specific learning needs.

Libraries may also run training in-house on many of the above, and you may find, depending upon your individual learning style, that attending one or more of these may increase your skills and confidence more quickly than using online tutorials.

The hope is that not only will you produce a dissertation that helps you to gain a good degree but that you will learn skills of information literacy that you will be able to use again and again both in your academic and professional careers.

Your supervisor

Do not forget that your supervisor is there to help you as well. They are likely to have expertise in your area and will be able to point you in the direction of some good initial sources. As you build your database of documents, check with your supervisor that you are going in the right direction. You should also share any new references that you find; supervisors will be pleased if you come across references that they have not seen before.

Your supervisor will also be able to give you advice as to how you can best structure your literature review.

> As my dissertation supervisor specialized in my area of interest, she was able to provide me with some useful references to get started with.

Key messages

- Smart searching is key to success.
- Remind yourself of the basics. Maybe you did a library induction at the start of your course two or three years ago and did not take in all the information that was not relevant then but is now.
- Be systematic in your search and keep a note of everything that you find.
- Make use of the full range of support available to you from within your institution and go and talk to your subject librarian.

Key questions

- Do you have the right skills in order to be able to search for material online (journals, databases, etc.)?
- If not, where can you get access to such support within your own institution?
- Are you familiar with what your own library offers – online resources, books, journals, audio-visual material, etc.?
- What support does the library offer in terms of help with finding literature and other research (training courses, individual support)?
- Have you defined your research clearly enough in order to construct search strategies that return sources relevant to your research?

Further reading

Gash, S. (2000) *Effective Literature Searching for Research*, Aldershot: Gower.
Hart, C. (1998) *Doing a Literature Review: Releasing the Social Science Research Imagination*, London: Sage.
Hart, C. (2001) *Doing a Literature Search: A Comprehensive Guide for the Social Sciences*, London: Sage.
Ó Dochartaigh, N. (2007) *Internet Research Skills: How to Do Your Literature Search and Find Research Information Online*, London: Sage.

Chapter 5

Designing your research methodology

Introduction

This chapter outlines options and related issues to help you choose the research methodology for your dissertation. We discuss some of the theoretical ideas that shape concepts and models to do with research methods in the social sciences. We show you that research is a complex and 'messy' business with lots of questions and issues to consider. However, we also want to show you how to think through these complexities without feeling overwhelmed. We want to give you information to help you feel confident to develop a research strategy suited to your question(s). Designing a research strategy necessitates a systematic and rigorous approach but one that is sufficiently flexible to be responsive to the resolution of tensions inherent in the actual practice of doing the research.

By the end of the chapter, you will have a better understanding of:

* research paradigms;
* research approaches and methods used in the social sciences;
* how to justify your strategy.

Brannen (2005) talks about the 'three Ps' that influence your rationale for your choice of methods and these will be introduced in this chapter:

1 paradigms;
2 pragmatics;
3 politics.

Research paradigms and philosophical positions

Your research strategy has a direct relationship to the type of research question that you formulate (Van der Velde *et al.* 2004). Such a strategy may be based upon one or a combination of the two dominant research paradigms: qualitative and quantitative (Collis and Hussey 2003; Johnson and Duberley 2000). Not only are these paradigms often associated with specific methodological approaches but they are also rooted in particular philosophies about the nature of evidence and how and why particular forms of evidence may be privileged in the research process. In essence, these relate to interpretivist and positivist views of the world, broadly meaning the extent to which understanding and meaning are derived using objective or subjective criteria.

The social sciences encompass a broad range of disciplines. Ideas about research, therefore, are contested across these disciplines, and different views are privileged at different times by different groups of researchers in different parts of the world. So research itself is political in nature. Feminist researchers, active since the 1970s, argue that research is a political activity and see the need to bring issues of power and gendered relations to the fore in articulating the nature and purpose of the research process (Campbell and Wasco 2000).

You do not need to get immersed in these debates to write your dissertation, but it is useful to engage with them and to understand their links with the need to justify your choice of research strategy and specific methods. Unfortunately, 'simple and straightforward' are not terms that can often be used when it comes to social research. 'Even those who aim to keep it simple for as long as possible are finally confronted with the ideas that they must write about their methodology and that this means more than "what I did"' (Dunne *et al.* 2005: 1).

Factors that may influence your methodological approach

Dissertations can make use of either quantitative or qualitative data, a combination of both, or they may combine different qualitative methods or different quantitative methods. Your choice may depend on your preferences and abilities and the suitability of particular approaches to your chosen topic. You need to be able to justify why you have chosen to use such an approach.

Don't mix too many methods together in such a small space. Using five different methods will not get you more marks if they don't contribute to the overall research findings.

Your preferred philosophical approach

As a first-time researcher, it is helpful if you recognize your own preferences and values – your axiology – because these will influence how you collect data, how you organize it and how you analyse it. Yet, you may not realize how what you are doing is mediated through your personal frame of reference. If you recognize this possibility at the start of your research, however, you have a better chance of being a better researcher. Thinking about the way you and others may see the world differently can help you when choosing your approach and can help you to critique the notions of positivism and interpretivism introduced at the start of the chapter and their relevance to developing a methodology. These ideas are connected with epistemological questions that address the production, scope and nature of knowledge, which shape research and scholarly processes and activities. Here are some examples of epistemological perspectives that impact research.

- Realism is linked to ontology and the naming and describing of existence. It is concerned with reality as observable and there being an existence that can be categorized and described, although critical realists would acknowledge that the observation of that reality is subjective in nature.
- Phenomenology always asks the question 'What is the nature or meaning of something?' and seeks to describe things as they present to us. It encompasses a number of traditions and orientations such as realistic, hermeneutic and existential (Embree 1997).
- Constructivism as a form of interpretivism asserts that meaning itself is contested and that this is because 'reality' is created through the filter of our own lived experiences and knowledge so that it is not an externally driven process but is personally mediated. Feminist researchers have used this to inform the development of a research paradigm that makes explicit the humanness of the researcher and the researched. Their stance suggests that researchers must engage in a critical reflexivity in order to make explicit the subjective and contested nature of meaning-making in research.

So what does this mean for your dissertation work? To help you think about these ideas a bit more, look at Figure 5.1. What do you see? What do you think is going on?

Your answer will depend partly upon the lens through which you are viewing the picture: your background, culture, race and experience. You will use this lens in your research, and you may find that it changes

Figure 5.1 What do you see?

sometimes. You are likely to have shades of preference, and you should not feel that they are fixed. Importantly, perhaps, you should feel comfortable with understanding and managing *pluralism* in relation to research, at all stages from design to dissemination.

You may feel a little confused about the significance of these ideas to your project, so reading further may help as might talking to your supervisor or other tutors. Logging the fact that research is complex and contested may be sufficient to inform your thinking and actions as you progress your work. Table 5.1 (Cresswell 2003: 5) shows the ways in which different assumptions underpinning research may shape the formation of the research question and the design of the research strategy.

Will your research be inductive or deductive?

Brannen (2005: 13) suggests that, when designing a research strategy, 'first a logic of enquiry drives the study'. In general, deductive research is theory-testing, and inductive research is theory-generating. Often people link:

- deductive research with quantitative experiments or surveys – focused on testing hypotheses;
- inductive research with qualitative interviews or ethnographic work – enquiry and discovery-focused.

Table 5.1 How assumptions underpinning research inform the question posed (Cresswell 2003)

Assumption	Question	Quantitative	Qualitative
Ontological assumption	What is the nature of reality?	Reality is objective and singular, apart from the researcher	Reality is subjective and multiple as seen by participants in a study
Epistemological assumption	What is the relationship of the researcher to that being researched?	Researcher is independent from that being researched	Researcher interacts with that being researched
Axiological assumption	What is the role of values?	Value-free and unbiased	Value-laden and biased
Rhetorical assumption	What is the language of research?	Formal Based on set definitions Impersonal voice Use of accepted quantitative words	Informal Evolving decisions Personal voice Accepted qualitative words
Methodological assumption	What is the process of research?	Deductive process	Inductive process

These links are not hard and fast; for instance, experimental research, designed to test a particular theory through developing a hypothesis and creating an experimental design, may use quantitative or qualitative data or a combination of the two. If your research starts with a theory and is driven by hypotheses that you are testing (e.g. that social class background and social deprivation or privilege are likely to affect educational attainment), it is, broadly speaking, deductive; however, much research combines deductive and inductive elements.

My advice is always think of the question; the question itself stipulates a kind of methodology to be used. Methodology can be the driving factor, but often it's the question that can be the driving factor.

Linking your skills and abilities with methods of data collection and analysis

Linked with your personal values that inform your view of the world may be the extent to which you want to use the research task to build on your existing skills or to take the opportunity to explore new skills. For example:

• Do you like talking to people?
• Do you feel confident about going to new places?
• Do you enjoy working with numbers?
• Would you have any special requirements for using certain approaches?

In the UK, universities have a legal responsibility to ensure equality of opportunity for disabled students, and, if you have specific access needs, you should discuss these with your supervisor or other supporters at an early stage so that support can be planned for and provided.

Your answers will help you think about which research methods you might wish to use, though you will also need to consider practical issues and the constraints or opportunities these may provide. These are discussed further in Chapter 6.

> My research design was massively influenced by other studies that I had found interesting to read and also methodological literature and its various discussions of which methodologies are appropriate where and why. Obviously, at undergraduate level, I was constrained by timing and funding issues as well.

What approach will you use?

When considering your research question and the time and resources available to you for your research, you have three options to consider for your dissertation. The first two will involve empirical work, which means handling data you gather yourself, including data that did not originate from your own work.

1   Primary research: do I want to collect original data for my dissertation?
2   Secondary research: do I want to utilize data from existing research?
3   Theoretical based: do I want to focus upon a literature-based piece of work?

Use of the third may be dependent upon the requirements stipulated for your dissertation module.

When you have made the decision about which type of research to adopt, you will then be able to consider which sort of approach will be suitable.

> My research design was structured by the content of the dissertation. A literature review was encouraged, not only due to the wealth of information out there on the subject but also because doing empirical analysis is sometimes considered too time consuming for undergraduates.

Conducting primary research

You need to carefully consider the advantages and disadvantages of primary data collection. Some advantages of primary data collection include the following:

- You are in control of the data collection and it is specific to your project.
- Your data will, therefore, be original.
- You will have intimate knowledge of your data and 'own' it.

Disadvantages may include the following:

- It is time consuming to do.
- Your data collection method(s) might not initially go to plan.
- You might generate a very small dataset to analyse.

Doing secondary research

Secondary research involves collating and analysing data generated by another researcher. It allows you to explore areas of interest without having to go through the fieldwork process yourself. Many students think about undertaking primary research, and yet the benefits of using existing high-quality data or literature are many and, in the context of increasingly demanding ethical requirements, might be considered as a first option rather than as a compromise second. Using fieldwork methods in an undergraduate dissertation is also often costly in terms of time and possibly your own financial resources. We recommend, therefore, that you explore seriously the option to undertake secondary research, analysing existing data.

Case study: how the media can be a fruitful source of data for undergraduate research

Rationale: The media can provide a wealth of material for you to use in preparation for your dissertation and is an interesting topic in itself. The media has an important role in constructing the social world in which we live. It helps to establish dominant agendas in society by creating or reinforcing dominant values and by marginalizing certain causes, or sections of society.

Research design issues: If you are interested in investigating the role of the media in society, it is useful to begin by identifying the broad approach you want to take.

- *The portrayal approach.* How is a section of society or an issue portrayed in the media? This will involve conducting a detailed examination of media content. If you are interested in newspapers, documentaries, films or music, this is probably the way to approach your research.
- *The impact approach.* What effect do newspapers, documentaries, etc., have upon the way we view a section of society or an issue? This will involve asking people through questionnaires, interviews or focus groups their views on the influence of the media. If you are interested in the impact of the media, this approach will probably be more suitable.

By concentrating upon the media, it is possible to explore a vast array of perspectives on any issue that you find of interest. Research methods tutors on your course or your supervisor will be able to advise on the availability and accessibility of such data sets.

(Gary Taylor)

Doing secondary analysis, particularly if you are doing a quantitative study, may enable you to work with much larger data sets than you could have collected yourself. This has the following advantages (based on work by Bryman 2004):

- They allow you to discuss trends and social changes.
- The data are often collected through a random sample, which allows you to generalize to the population under consideration.
- The data is usually of a high quality.
- They may also allow you to make comparisons over time, as some datasets are products of longitudinal studies.

Secondary analysis has some disadvantages:

*   The data were collected for a purpose different from yours.
*   You have to find out something about that purpose, as well as the methods of collection, in order to justify your use of a secondary data set.

Overall, you need to think carefully about the advantages and disadvantages of secondary analysis in terms of your own research questions.

Theory-based and other literature-based projects

A literature-based or theoretical study is not necessarily 'easier' than an empirical study: indeed, it may well be harder and, again, should not be considered a 'second best' option to undertaking primary work, although in some programmes this may be a requirement. Remember that theoretical studies, like data-based studies, need to have their research design spelled out from the start.

These will usually be entirely literature-based. The methodology of theoretical analysis is likely to include selection and discussion of theoretical material and descriptive material, in context, and detailed comparison of theories in terms of their applicability. You might ask how useful certain concepts or theories are for understanding particular patterns of behaviour or for predicting outcomes.

*   How useful is the concept of institutional racism?
*   Is objectivity in the media possible?
*   How useful is subcultural theory for understanding virtual communities?

Here, the focus of attention is not so much to discover something about the social world, for example, virtual communities, as to reach a judgement about the value of key concepts or theories in understanding that world. How the study is approached and how contrasting approaches are chosen needs to be stated very clearly.

Even if your dissertation is more empirically focused, it could still be entirely literature-based. You might choose to conduct a review of existing research related to a particular topic. What does the research literature in this field tell us about *antisocial behaviour*, for example? While all dissertations will include a literature review, it is possible to produce a dissertation that is entirely based on a review of the literature, for example, looking at the various discourses about youth crime in different countries (see Chapter 4).

Overview of methods

In this section, we introduce some examples of specific approaches to research which are used in the social sciences. A culture of cross-disciplinarity and inter-disciplinarity in the social sciences has paved the way for promoting methodological adaptation and developments within and across disciplines. We caution you that within each approach there will be a number of variants as researchers use, critique and adapt them. We encourage you to draw on ideas and principles to inform your methodology as the scale of your dissertation means that you will not be able to apply a full-blown application of many of the approaches.

Case-study approaches

Case-study research can be well suited to an undergraduate dissertation. This approach to research uses a narrow lens to build a rich or thick description of a single group, organization or individual. A case study may utilize different kinds of data to build this picture, including interview material, observation and documentary analysis. The emphasis is on representing an accurate picture of the individual case and does not seek to propose generalizable results. Case studies can be used on their own or as part of a combined approach to data collection. Case-study research is often used in social work and education.

Evaluation research

Weiss (1998: 4) defines evaluation as 'systematic assessment of the operation and/or the outcomes of a program or policy, compared to a set of explicit or implicit standards, as a means of contributing to the improvement of the program or policy'. Evaluations usually involve discussions between researchers and programme providers to define the focus of the evaluation and the methods to be used that meet the needs of both groups. Evaluations use a range of methods and commonly adopt mixed-methods approaches, requiring both descriptive data and data that identify 'hard' outcomes, often represented numerically. As an undergraduate, if you are on a course in which work placements are involved, you may have the opportunity to contribute to evaluative activity in a small way. Given the timescales involved, you would probably need to focus upon a discrete aspect or period in the delivery of a programme, for example, within an educational, community or social welfare setting. Evaluation research, given its applied nature, is used often in social work, education, community work and social policy.

Ethnography

The American Anthropological Association (2004, online) states that 'ethnography involves the researcher's study of human behaviour in the natural settings in which people live', while the Open University (online) describes researchers' use of ethnography 'to get "inside" social worlds, to see these "through the eyes" of research subjects and to understand and explain these worlds in all their richness, complexity and specificity'.

Ethnographic studies utilize a range of methods including observation, interviews, documentary analysis and analysis of visual and other media. While associated with anthropological studies, ethnographic approaches are used by researchers across a range of disciplines including education, sociology and health. Ethnography is undoubtedly interesting to many but within the scope of an undergraduate dissertation it is likely that you will undertake a mini-ethnography (Sussman and Gilgun 1997), which involves the use of ethnographic ideas to shape the design of your questions and approach to data collection to construct a 'doable' project.

Action research

Action research situates the researcher as an insider, rather than the traditional 'outsider' position and is often deployed, therefore, by practitioners, for example, in education, health or social work settings. As the term implies, action research is concerned with the action that results from the research process and the impact of conducting the research. Key to this is a reflective cycle, which frames the research as an iterative, negotiated process *with* research participants from which findings emerge and inform change often both during and after the research. Examples of popular use of action research include:

• Participatory action research, as a variant, is often used in community-development work, community-health projects and development work in southern countries. In addition to the elements of action research, it is also concerned with a redistribution of power between the researcher and research participants who are seen as partners in the process (Baum *et al.* 2006). Sharing planning, data collection and negotiating the nature and significance of that data as well as engaging in action from the research involves time and dedication, yet this is integral to this approach.

• Professional practice. Action research is commonly used when undertaking classroom-based research and exploring other areas of professional practice. Newman (2000) identifies two perspectives informing action research in this context: Schön's (1983) idea of enquiry-based practice as an embedded approach for informing changes to practice and North's (1987) as emerging from a specific problem or question requiring attention.

As a researcher, this action research poses challenges for thinking about appropriate boundaries in research and the use of self, one of the reasons for research being by necessity a reflective activity. It can also be very time-consuming because you are not working alone; you are accommodating the interests and timescales of others who are part of the research activity.

Visual methods

The British Sociological Society's Visual Sociology group identifies three approaches encompassed by visual sociology (www.visualsociology.org.uk online, 2008):

1 data collection using video cameras and other recording technology;
2 studying visual data produced by cultures;
3 communication with images and media other than words.

The International Visual Sociology Association (2008) describes the artefacts used in visual sociology as still photographs, film, video and electronically transmitted images for the following purposes:

• documentary studies of everyday life in contemporary communities;
• the interpretive analysis of art and popular visual representations of society;
• studies of the messages, meanings and social impact of advertising and the commercial use of images;
• the analysis of archival images as sources of data on society and culture;
• the study of the purpose and meaning of image-making such as recreational and family photography and videography.

Visual and communications technologies play an increasingly important role in many people's everyday lives; therefore, the use of methods associated with visual sociology or ethnography offer relevant and interesting routes to capturing and analysing data. However, understanding the analytical tools associated with such methods may involve a lot of time, practice and study. So, what might appear to be easy and accessible data may pose challenges at a later stage in the research.

Experimental research

Although more commonly associated with the physical sciences, experimental and quasi-experimental research is also utilized in the social sciences, particularly in psychology. Experimental research involves controlled conditions that may be replicated and is often, though not exclusively, conducted in laboratory conditions. Developments in this field are often interdisciplinary and concerned with understanding how policy interventions designed to change human behaviour may be implemented without coercion and high costs. There are many research centres in the USA, for example, devoted to such research, and if you were interested in this type of research you would need to identify the availability of appropriate resources to enable you to conduct your experiments. This type of research usually generates quantitative data.

Policy research

The complex and ever-changing policy landscape (health, education, social care, communities) invites the need for evidence-based approaches to policy design and review. The interface between social lives, political drivers and policy formation at local to national level provides fertile ground for student researchers to undertake reviews of policy or to explore comparative questions (policy reform across time or countries), supported by the availability of material published by government departments, campaigning organizations and others.

Pragmatics: justifying your approach

Any piece of research needs to justify its methods. You need to show in the dissertation how you considered different methods and why you chose or eliminated these. You are advised to spend some time exploring books and literature about research methods: they will give you an overview of the data-collection methods available and help you to make the best choice for your project. See the reading list at the end of this chapter for ideas.

Research has shown (Todd *et al.* 2006: 167) that supervisors saw part of their role as being to tease out their students' reasons for choosing a particular research approach. Often, in early supervision meetings, they got their students to justify their reasons for choosing a library-based or an empirical study. Your supervisor will want you to be able to come up with some convincing reasons as to why you have chosen the approach you have – so be ready.

If you are having difficulty making that choice, don't be afraid to ask your supervisor for his or her advice. This was particularly useful for one of our respondents.

> I wouldn't have known what research method to use on my own – I needed the tutor for this. You need to see your tutor before you're able to start work on it.

This chapter has covered the broad considerations in designing a research strategy. Chapter 6 looks in more detail at specific techniques and traditions of use within different social science disciplines.

Key messages

- Research is political in nature, and ideas and positions are contested and contestable.
- Think about and acknowledge your own value and preferences in relation to evidence and approaches.
- It is vital that your approach is appropriate to your question and topic.
- Undertaking secondary research or theoretical projects should not be seen as second best to doing primary research – all present opportunities and challenges.
- Adopt an approach that will fit with the time, resources and interest available to you. Remember, research is a greedy animal and will eat up your time and resources.
- Whatever approach you settle on, you *must* be able to justify its appropriateness to your topic and question.

Key questions

- What do you think about the arguments related to subjectivity/objectivity in research, and what some would argue is a false dualism that is often associated with these arguments?

- Which approach will best enable you to generate data appropriate to your question?
- What factors may limit the scope of your research (time, resources, etc.)?
- Do you know the implications of choosing particular approaches at different stages of your research?
- Do you feel confident that you can justify your approach in a logical, coherent and reasoned way?
- Have you sought guidance and advice from your supervisor or tutor?

Further reading

Bryman, A. (2004) *Social Research Methods*, 2nd edn, Oxford: Oxford University Press.

Creswell, J. (2003) *Research Design: Qualitative, Quantitative, and Mixed Methods Approaches*, 2nd edn, London: Sage.

Denscombe, M. (2003) *The Good Research Guide for Small-Scale Social Research Projects*, Maidenhead: Open University Press.

Dunne, M., Pryor, J. and Yates, P. (2005) *Becoming a Researcher: A Research Companion for the Social Sciences*, Maidenhead: Open University Press.

Gerring, J. (2007) *Case Study Research: Principles and Practices*, Cambridge: Cambridge University Press.

Rose, G. (2002) *Visual Methodologies*, London: Sage.

Seale, C. (2006) *Researching Society and Culture*, London: Sage.

Yin, R. K. (2003) *Case Study Research, Design and Methods*, 3rd edn, Newbury Park, Calif.: Sage Publications.

Chapter 6

Data collection

Introduction

When you have considered and chosen your research methodology, as explored in the previous chapter, you will want to decide which data-collection techniques to use and plan how and when you will collect your data. You will then undertake the fieldwork, which is a challenging but usually very interesting part of the research process. Planning is key to undertaking and managing data collection, so this chapter will help you to think through some of the issues and practicalities associated with responsible and rigorous data collection. Analysis of your data is covered in Chapters 8 and 9 but forms an important part of the planning stage needed before embarking on your data collection, so we advise you to read both chapters together.

By the end of this chapter, you will have a better understanding of:

- techniques of data collection;
- data-collection dos and don'ts.

Data-collection techniques

There are many ways of gathering both quantitative and qualitative data in a systematic, rigorous and accountable way. In this section, we introduce you to a range of techniques to enable you to consider preferences to explore further with your supervisor, to inform your reading of research-methods literature and reviews of existing research.

Many students may think of either survey techniques or interviews as a first option, and we want to invite you to consider a broader range of techniques that may fit well within the requirements and expectations of an undergraduate programme of study. Lee (2000: 1) discusses the benefits of unobtrusive methods that refer to 'data gathered by means that do not involve direct elicitation of information from research subjects', for example what he terms 'physical traces' through the evidence people leave behind them. We want to encourage you to think about the rich seam of possibilities for answering a range of questions through the use of trace evidence as your main data source. In selecting technique(s) you will want to ensure that the option(s) you choose will:

- generate data that will answer your question(s) both in terms of the size of the data set (neither too large nor too small) and quality;
- fit the resources available to you (time, skills, access, costs).

Beissel-Durrant (2004: 11) presents one approach for creating a typology of research methods in the social sciences and sets out categories of techniques. These are shown in Table 6.1, to which we have added suggestions for when they might be appropriate to deploy.

You may be interested in doing an analysis that is primarily quantitative, looking at social trends or policy implications. However, you also want to introduce a 'human touch' by conducting one or several interviews asking what these trends mean to people or how particular individuals experience events. After doing your quantitative analysis, you should include a chapter or section on the qualitative data you have collected. In your discussion of findings, you can use the qualitative data to help you understand the patterns in the quantitative analysis.

> Semi-structured interviews worked well in both of my dissertations, particularly where good rapport was generated with participants. Diary entries also proved useful, but there was more scope for misunderstanding of task requirements here, as obviously I was not present when the diaries were being completed.

Table 6.1 Categories of data-collection techniques and reasons to use them

Category	Useful for . . .
Interviewing	Gathering the views of a wide range of people, for example if you wanted to get people's views on their experience of using a drop-in facility for street homelessness, you will be more likely to get users' views by interviewing them than by leaving questionnaires for people to self-complete.

continued

Questionnaires	Gathering the views of lots of people in a standardized way, helpful if questions are non-sensitive (e.g. use of local public transport) or very sensitive (e.g. spending habits in relation to personal income levels) so people may appreciate the anonymity. With responses you can count, measure and score views and compare responses by variables and across data sets – enabling you to undertake a range of statistical analyses.
Observation	Helpful for understanding and measuring behaviours and actions, for instance, in the example about the drop-in centre you could sit in the centre and observe how people are using it. This is less obtrusive than interviewing.
Measurement	Useful for identifying change at different points in time, for example, pre and post intervention (e.g. therapy) and often with the use of standardized assessment instruments, common in psychology and education.
Use of administrative sources	Collating and analysing data that is generated, for example, through routine work activities so that material gathered for one purpose can be utilized for a second, as research data. This may include case records of users of social care services, minutes of meetings and attendance records.
Visual methods	There are variations but these can enable participants to self-report (by capturing their own photographs or video) or the researcher can capture a set of materials and then engage in joint or individual analysis of their meaning and significance.
New technologies	The internet has opened up lots of possibilities for gathering primary and secondary data and for reaching specific populations, through, for example, content analysis of discussion board messages or statistical analysis of hits on different web sites or pages. Again, depending upon what you do, there may be a range of ethical issues to consider such as those related to personal boundaries, privacy issues and online identities.
	Mobile technologies also provide new ways of gathering primary data or sourcing secondary data for analysis such as text-messaging and its impact on social relations and global positioning systems for tracking movements (e.g. routes taken by community members to help to identify how to maximize community safety with street lighting, open spaces, etc.).

Some possible advantages and disadvantages of different techniques

Each of the modes of data collection highlighted above present their own advantages and disadvantages. You might wish to consider these and see if any of them might sway your decision to use or not use a particular technique. Also, for each technique, you usually have options to consider, for example, one-to-one or group interviews. Some of the modes of deployment for interviews are shown in Figure 6.1 and for survey administration in Figure 6.2. Some of the options may not be suitable for particular populations or because of the resources available to you. Some pros and cons associated with these modes are highlighted next, but you may be able to identify others for your own research situation to aid your decision-making.

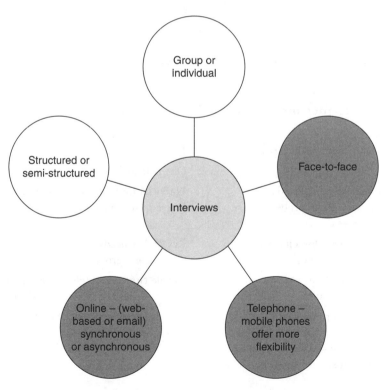

Figure 6.1 Interview modes.

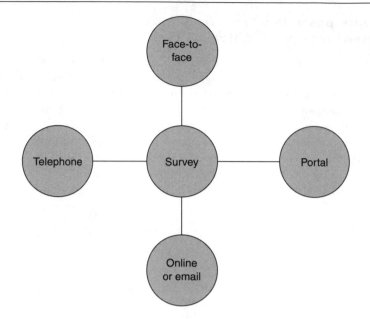

Figure 6.2 Modes of survey administration.

Face-to-face interviews – individual or group

Pros

Engagement with respondent(s)

Flexible

Rich data is collected and interviewer can probe answers and delve deeper

Sometimes allows for discussion of sensitive issues

Able to pick up and respond to non-verbal cues

Focus groups allow for the views of many to be gathered at one session – sharing of views and experiences may enrich the data collected

Cons

Journey time and costs

One person's view is just that

Potential for unequal participation in group interviews

Researcher needs to be confident in managing a group situation

Ample time needs to be allowed for transcription and collation of data

Not usually appropriate for sensitive topics

Telephone interviewing

Pros	Cons
Cheaper than face-to-face	Non-verbal cues hard to pick up
Quality of data is improved if time/ date to conduct interview is arranged in advance and interviewees see questions below	Some people not comfortable or able to talk on the phone
Tele-conferencing is possible with small numbers	Tele-conferencing difficult to manage with numbers greater than two to three
	May be hard to check out reasons for silence

Online interviews via asynchronous text chat including email

Pros	Cons
Respondent has time to consider answers	Conversational style is restricted
Immediate capture of text data	Time-lapses may mean important response threads are lost

Online interviews via synchronous chat

Pros	Cons
May help to put some users at ease, for example, young people, or when discussing sensitive topics	Lacks personal engagement
Immediate capture of text data	Reliant on good enough typing speeds of researcher and interviewee
Can keep digging deeper into answers	May be difficult to get in-depth answers
	Endings need to be managed

Interviews conducted via web cams or videoconferencing

Pros	Cons
Closest proximity to face-to-face conversation	Digital divide – access by potential interviewees
Bridges problems created by geographical distance	May experience time delays in giving and receiving sound, thus stilting discussion
Group (or individual) interviews possible but practicalities may mean maximum four to five for a group is workable	Technology may not be reliable

Surveys

Surveys completed by or in presence of researcher, including telephone

Pros	Cons
Researcher has more control over completion rates	Sample number likely to be smaller
Can access answers from those who may not be able to read a questionnaire or complete answers	Respondents may feel obliged to respond or if they receive a telephone request 'cold' may be suspicious
	Types of questions that can be asked may be limited due to lack of privacy and/or direct questioning

Postal surveys

Pros	Cons
Can reach larger numbers and resources involved can be measured quite easily	Postage costs, including costs of return postage and administration time (stuffing envelopes)
Can reach dispersed samples	May need to do several follow-ups to generate target number of returns
	Literacy of respondents

Questionnaires sent via email – embedded or as attachment

Pros	Cons
Can reach larger numbers and low cost	Access of respondents to email
Can reach dispersed samples	May need to do several follow-ups to generate enough responses
Suited to large numbers of replies	Literacy of respondents

Online survey tools

Pros	Cons
Can reach larger numbers and low cost	Access of respondents to email
Can reach dispersed samples	May need to do several follow-ups to generate enough responses
Suited to large numbers of replies	Literacy of respondents
No collation stage involved	Costs if you cannot access free software

General issues with surveys

- Can reach large numbers of respondents.
- Statistical analyses can be applied.
- Design stage needs to be thorough – work is frontloaded.
- May be viewed as somewhat depersonalized but this may be helpful for some topic areas and with some groups of respondents.

Flexibility and consistency

You might think these two words contradict each other, so let us explain each of them a little more in relation to doing research. Designing a research strategy necessitates a systematic and rigorous approach but one that is sufficiently flexible to be responsive to the resolution of tensions inherent in the actual practice of doing the research. In other words, what you planned and hoped to do may not always be possible because 'life happens', as the next quote from one student illustrates.

> I developed a health problem, which was sufficient to interrupt my work schedule. After discussion with my supervisor, it was agreed that the second stage of the research (which would have involved some quantitative analysis) would not be carried out and the dissertation would focus on the qualitative analysis, which had already been conducted.

If you are undertaking research and you are trying to answer a particular set of questions, it helps to apply the same routine to eliciting answers from people. This will increase your chances of getting the types of answers you are hoping for and also lend credibility to your research.

However, issues and problems often occur when conducting research, and you need to be prepared for and able to accommodate unexpected events. For example, people may cancel interviews, you may experience low response rates to a survey or weather can affect travelling plans to fieldwork sites – the possibilities are endless. Therefore, it is useful to have contingency plans in these circumstances.

If you anticipate or have problems with data collection that may impact on the data you hoped to gather or have the potential to affect completion of your study, speak to your supervisor as early as possible. This will increase your chances of finding alternatives or managing the risk and impact on your study.

> You may be interested in doing an evaluative case study of a process or policy. You will have a particular focus – a 'case' – that you are looking at. You will triangulate methods – i.e. collect data in several different ways – and some of these data may be quantitative. You will analyse each type of data, describe this and then write a discussion that shows how each piece of analysis contributes to the overall picture of what is going on.

Order and weighting in combined approaches

If you decide to use a multi-method approach, collecting more than one set of data, you will need to plan the order in which you need to collect these. For example, a focus group interview may be used to assist in formulating appropriate questions and undertaken prior to the design of a survey. In addition to the order, you also want to assess the relative importance in your study of each set of data – understanding this will help you weight the time you spend on each appropriately.

Morse (2003) has a helpful way of quickly visually sequencing using capital letters and forward sign or plus sign for simultaneity:

QUAL > quan

In this example, qualitative data is collected first and represents more work and weighting at the analysis stage than the quantitative data that comes next, unlike the next example where they have equal emphasis.

QUAL > QUAN

QUAN > QUAL + QUAL

In this example, a quantitative method is used first, followed by collection of two sets of qualitative at the same time. All have equal dominance for analysis. There are lots of variations, including overlapping and concurrent data-collection activities.

Where do I find existing research data?

There is a wide range of sources that already provide research data (hard-copy text, online and multimedia) that you can analyse. In the UK, Intute (www.intute.ac.uk) is an online hub that provides a list of research sites including international data sources and archives accessible to the academic community, often free of charge, such as National Statistics Online and Qualidata in the UK, the Australian Social Science Data Archive, OFFSTATS, the University of Auckland Library and the US National Data Analysis System containing child-welfare-related datasets. Examples of other data sources include:

*   museums, art galleries and archives;
*   website of organizations and informal sources such as social networking sites (we say more about these in Chapter 7);
*   media such as newspapers, magazines, video or other media – even non-fiction books such as autobiographies;
*   reports and documentation – for example, internal material generated by organizations and government reports.

There is a grey area between analysing existing research data and utilizing material that has been produced but which has not yet been subjected to an external research lens, for example, annual reports of organizations. Similarly, case documentation and other routinely generated records exist already, but their use in research is for a different purpose than that which was originally intended. The important issue is to present the material you are using and how you are using it in a transparent way.

> The first step was to make contact with the professional body. As this was a documentary study, first contact was made with the person keeping the archive, namely the librarian, by making a phone call. This is often a good tactic because the whole thing can be kept in a low key, by explaining that you want to find out who to ask for permission to use the library. [...] The librarians who were so helpful in finding documentation were often able to help in another vital matter for this project, namely the freedom to photograph.
>
> (Macdonald 1993: 209)

Design of research instruments

Whether you plan to conduct a survey, undertake observational work or conduct interviews, you will be utilizing one or more 'research instruments' for collecting data. These might involve anything from a highly structured questionnaire designed to collect data that is quantitative and measurable to the researcher or a more flexible topic-focused interview schedule designed to elicit qualitative data of a descriptive textual nature.

You will need to think about whether your instrument is prestructured, open-ended or a combination of both. This refers to questions or categories of enquiry that are coded at the design stage or at the analysis stage.

In psychological studies, for example, you may adopt the use of a standardized instrument for assessment or other forms of measurement. If you are not using an 'off the shelf' instrument, then you will need to design your own questionnaire or question schedule or observation sheet.

Even if you are designing your own, it will help you if you spend some time looking for examples of instruments designed for other studies, including dissertations from previous years.

In particular, if you plan to use questions about respondent characteristics such as age, race or sex, you will be able to make use of the categories adopted in national surveys such as censuses. These ensure you are conforming to current practice with terminology.

We do not have the space in this section to provide an in-depth review of how to construct a valid research instrument for all situations. However, we do highlight some issues that you should explore further and explain why in many circumstances a piloting phase for the instruments is helpful, even if for you this means testing your instrument out with friends or fellow students.

When designing your instrument:

- Keep your research question to the forefront so your instrument will generate relevant data for finding an answer.
- Consider your mode of deployment and your audience or focus of enquiry (for example, if using observation) and how this may influence the design of your instrument. For instance, with self-administered instruments there can be little room for ambiguity, whereas a semi-structured interview schedule will allow for a teasing out of both an interviewee's understanding of the question and your understanding of their response.
- Which sorts of questions (open or closed questions or a combination of both) are likely to elicit the best and most accurate response?
- Have you considered carefully the structure of your questions so you are not leading the respondent to reply in a certain way?
- Order and type of questions – surveys may require a different kind of logic than an interview schedule, with the former inviting a 'mix 'em up' approach of question types and item options, the latter perhaps following a more conversational logic. For more details on question types and ordering, see our web pages on the Routledge website (www.routledge.com).
- Language and presentation should be appropriate to your target population. Check readability and accessibility, for example print size and colour. If you are scanning completed questionnaires for use with analysis software, this will influence their format.
- What is a reasonable time for completion? Interviewing an eight-year-old child in a classroom setting will require the design of a short instrument, but, if you are observing children's behaviours in that classroom, for how long do you think you could maintain your attention on the task?
- When doing interviews, try to have a few practice runs first, for example, with friends or housemates. This will get you oriented into the research situation and familiar with the process.

Sampling

Whatever approach you adopt, you will need to consider sampling issues. Sampling involves selection of a proportion of units, people, objects or artefacts upon which to focus your data collection from a larger set, group or population. It is important to seek guidance from your supervisor to assist you in understanding how to construct an appropriate sampling method for your research. The type of sample you choose will relate closely to your research methodology, to the population, objects or artefacts you are studying and will need to fit your resources and capacity. Big isn't always better in undergraduate dissertation sampling. A key thing to remember is to know your population and the audience you are trying to reach in your research.

A key question that often arises in applying sampling considerations relates to generalization, that is the extent to which findings generated from a specific sample or study can be generalized to a wider population, so are concerned with external validity. You may not be in a position or wish to construct a sample that leads to this kind of validity, but your conclusions should be supported by a theory-informed and well-executed process that are deemed reliable, and for experimental and comparative studies should be associated with internal validity. This is concerned with whether the process and assessments actually measure what you intended them to. We discuss some of the wider issues of responsible researchers and generalization in Chapter 7. You will need to read more widely to understand different ways to construct a sample and their different benefits and limitations in specific research contexts, but some of the common methods include:

- *Random sampling.* This involves selecting a sub-group from a homogeneous larger population through a process based on criteria that do not relate to any characteristics of the population (for example, choosing every fourth person or entry on a list).
- *Stratified sampling.* In a potential sample population, there may be particular characteristics or sub-groups you want to ensure are represented in your final sample. Stratification involves identifying these and then sampling from within these sub-groups. For example, you may have a class of children and you want to ensure that the 60/40-per cent split by sex is mirrored in your sample. So you would create a list of two sexes, then perhaps apply a random sampling approach to choosing your numbers within each of these two groups.
- *Clustering sampling.* Multi-stage sampling involves clustering what may appear to be naturally occurring groups within populations that are heterogeneous (for example, schools or electoral areas) in nature and then selecting a sample of these clusters randomly for inclusion in a study, with all units within each cluster included in the sample. So a simple example is schools in an electoral area are randomly sampled and pupils in the schools selected are the 'units of study'. All pupils would be sampled in each of the schools randomly selected. If these

units are subject to a further random selection stage; this would constitute multi-stage clustering, for example, the sampled units are derived from a random selection of girls in each of the schools.

• *Probability sampling.* This involves setting up a random sampling approach that ensures that ascribed population characteristics have an equal likelihood of being chosen.

• *Purposive or theoretical sampling.* These involve introducing an element of researcher selection into the sample. In undergraduate small-scale research, they may be utilized for practical purposes and are commonly associated with qualitative research, where validity is not based on ideas of representativeness. Theoretical sampling (Glaser and Strauss 1967; Strauss and Corbin 1998) involves the researcher making explicit the conceptual basis underlying the study. This makes conceptual generalization (understood as transferability) from one context to another a possibility.

Doing your research

In this section we offer practical suggestions associated with doing your research.

Being organized

The key to successful data collection is planning and organization. Different modes of data collection present different sorts of challenges and opportunities that impact on planning issues. For example, with surveys, a lot of the hard work is done at the design stage, formulating and testing the precision of questionnaire design, while qualitative methods involve a lot of work in collation and organizing after the data is collected.

You will need to put together a timetable for preparing for data collection including:

• organizing the work associated with data collection (e.g. contacting potential interview respondents and scheduling visits or survey administration, sorting ethical approval, printing any paperwork);

• working out timelines associated with collation, analysis and reporting of data so that you are aware of where there are possibilities to make up time if you experience any slippage with your data-collection timelines;

• maintaining an efficient and up-to-date filing and data storage system – both paper-based and on your computer for the management of data as you collect it;

- ensuring fieldwork notes or any other material such as video or digital photographs are dated and logged as they are collected – it is very easy to quickly misplace things or forget details;
- transcribing material as soon as possible so it is fresh in your mind;
- ensuring, if you have scheduled a pilot stage, that you maintain your milestones for this early stage – you do not want to be running behind through the rest of the project.

Arranging fieldwork visits

Arrange the dates and times of fieldwork or site visits as early as is possible and discuss your plans with your supervisor. Give as much information in advance as you are able to, but in a style and format that is appropriate to your audience. The next student quote shows the length of time involved in establishing trust with a hard-to-reach group before interviews could be undertaken.

> Homeless people are acknowledged as being difficult to reach, and, due to their transient nature, it is a challenge to seek prior consent or arrange interview times. Many are also extremely wary of someone new in their midst. I attended the GP clinic for several months and worked as a volunteer at one of the homeless shelters in order to maintain regular contact and build up trust among the client group in order to conduct enough interviews for the research analysis. In the end, only seven interviews were conducted over the next six months.

Correspondence, including draft email texts, should be checked whenever possible with your supervisor before sending out so that, for example, information letters and consent forms contain the correct information if your institution does not require you to use standardized documentation. Keep accurate records of your correspondence and communications; this will be of particular importance if you need to account for low response rates for requests for site visits and participation. You may need to make contact with sites in a number of ways to get a response, for example, by letter, email or telephone. Decide in advance how you will encourage potential participants to contribute to your research. Will you follow up your letters? How? When? What is a reasonable level of contact, and when should you assume silence means 'No'. There are no hard-and-fast rules here, so try to apply principles of fairness and reasonableness when deciding on a course of action.

When you have your visits confirmed, prepare thoroughly with your directions, transport linked with timings – so you arrive relaxed and in good time. Construct a list of all the things you need to take with you and do at the visit and afterwards, for example, sending thank-you letters.

Write down your itinerary and leave it with a colleague or friend so that they know where you should be and when. If you are concerned about confidentiality of your subjects, put their details into a sealed envelope and the details of your plans on the envelope so information need only be read in an emergency.

Many social service and health-care users have experiences of being kept waiting, and, to increase your chances of eliciting good data, you want them to be open and welcoming, not irritated by your lateness. If you are delayed, try and call in advance to let the relevant person know. Think carefully about to whom you should give your personal details, such as phone number. You may wish to keep your number hidden to the person you are calling if making contact using a personal telephone. In most situations, switch the phone off during the data-collection activity.

Risk assessment

You must consider your own safety when undertaking fieldwork and ensure you have addressed any potential risks. Completion of a risk-assessment form is common, and you should ask your supervisor about this if they do not raise it with you. Risk assessment is useful for thinking through the potential risks (however unlikely) that may arise when carrying out your research. You can then think through procedures for (a) minimizing those risks and (b) ensuring that you have contingency plans should they arise. Potential risks include the following:

- actual or threatened violence, psychological harm, unwanted sexual advances, etc.;
- injury travelling to or from the research venue;
- unfounded allegations are made against you (e.g. that you made sexual advances towards or threatened a participant);
- being implicated in illegal activities.

The site visit

When you arrive at the site, make yourself known and, if necessary, show a form of identification such as a student letter and any communications confirming the details of the visit. During the data-collection activities, depending upon the situation, think about where you are positioned. For example, for your own safety with some groups or individuals, you may consider sitting near the door with interviewees in front of you so that you are nearest to the exit. You should try and arrange interviews in public or semi-public places and avoid seeing people in their private homes. If you can only arrange interviews in the evening, take additional precautions.

If at any point during an interview you feel uncomfortable or unsafe, do not hesitate to end the interview and leave – listen to your feelings. If you are feeling sufficiently uncomfortable, this means you are unlikely to be able to elicit data effectively anyway.

You have thought about your own needs and safety in the planning process. In addition to the ethical issues covered in Chapter 7, you also need to think about the comfort and safety of your research participants, to be considerate in the way you approach your data collection.

It may help you to think about the data-collection process from the participants' perspective.

- What concerns might they have?
- What do they need to know in advance of completing a questionnaire or being interviewed?
- What issues might be similar or different if you are talking with them alone to talking with someone as part of a group?
- What do you think they would like to happen afterwards?

Tools and equipment

The range of kit available to assist you with data collection is increasing as technology becomes cheaper, smaller and more sophisticated in function. This supports the use of web-based tools and mobile devices such as laptops, PDAs, cameras, MP3 and MP4 recorders and players as well as mobile phones. Obvious tips for use include:

- ensuring your equipment is fully charged and/or has working batteries before you go;
- taking spare batteries;
- testing the quality and range of your recording/filming devices;
- having a back-up plan in case circumstances change and you have to revert to traditional methods such as pen and paper.

Key messages

- There are many different methods and techniques for collecting data, both quantitative and qualitative.
- All methods have strengths and limitations, so use a method that is a good fit for your question and situation.
- Efficient and effective planning and organization are crucial to ensure you remember all the things you need to do and within the timescales you have set for this phase of work.
- Consult with your supervisor in the design of your research instrument(s) and sampling. Confirm that it's OK to use questions from other studies (with appropriate acknowledgement).
- Make a checklist of all the practical tasks you have to do.

Key questions

- Have you explored different data-collection options?
- Have you chosen techniques appropriate to your question, skills and resources available to you, including time?
- Have you appreciated the potential value of secondary sources, rather than privileging primary data?
- Is your detailed planning in hand to ensure you can complete your fieldwork in good time to analyse and report on the data you collected?

Further reading

Angrosino, M. (2006) *Doing Cultural Anthropology: Projects for Ethnographic Data Collection*, 2nd edn, Long Grove, Ill.: Waveland Press.

Gilbert, N. (ed.) (1993) *Researching Social Life*, London: Sage.

Gorard, S. and Taylor, C. (2004) *Combining Methods in Educational and Social Research*, Maidenhead: Open University Press.

Lee, R. (2000) *Unobtrusive Methods in Social Research*, Buckingham: Open University Press.

Chapter 7

Research ethics and being a responsible researcher

Introduction

Previous chapters of this book have addressed some of the practical and conceptual issues connected with planning your dissertation. In this chapter, ethical principles and the practicalities of applying these principles in carrying out good social research are explored to help you to conduct your research in an ethical manner. We begin the chapter by explaining why matters of ethics are so central to the research process and then show you how to ensure you meet ethical requirements when carrying out research, from a principled stance to meeting formal ethical guidelines required by your institution and other related organizations. While the formal requirements and expectations may differ dependent upon the country you live in, there are understandings and rules of good social research of which all those undertaking such research must be cognisant, although in an increasingly globalized research landscape there is a need to debate and refine such rules. By the end of the chapter, you will have more information and ideas about:

- the importance of ethics in social research;
- ethical principles and morals;
- ethics and practicalities in research;
- being a responsible researcher.

What do we mean by research ethics?

The terms 'ethics' and 'morals' tend to be used interchangeably. Francis (1999) makes a useful distinction between the two:

- *Ethics* generally refer to a written code of value principles that we use in a particular context.

- *Morals* generally refer to an unwritten set of values that provide a frame of reference that we use to help our decision-making and regulate our behaviour.

Research ethics are, therefore, the principles that we use to make decisions about what is acceptable practice in any research project. Issues of morality are related to the behaviours and attitudes you might adopt in your approach to data collection and how you use your research.

Why is ethical research important?

Research participants have moral and legal rights, and it is important that as researchers we do not violate these rights. We have to be careful that our enthusiasm for getting answers to our research questions does not lead us to pay less attention to the informed involvement of the research participant or co-researcher than we should. A code of research ethics provides an agreed standard of activity for researchers, which is designed to protect participants' moral and legal rights at every stage of the research.

A code of research ethics also promotes quality in research as it is essential for the public to trust the results of research, given that findings may impact significantly on their lives. Having researchers conform to codes of research ethics helps to protect against harmful, poor or dishonest research practice, including in the representation of results. It is unfortunate that there are renowned examples of individuals failing to act in a principled way that had dire consequences for those subjects of the research, including the actions of Nazi doctors in the Second World War in concentration camps, which, in part, was a motivating factor in the development of the Helsinki Declaration, discussed in the next section.

What are the basic principles for ethical research?

The Economic and Social Research Council (ESRC) produced a Research Ethics Framework in 2006 to which all research it funded was required to comply. The framework acknowledges the diversity of the social sciences, and this means the ethical issues and complexities associated with different studies may vary considerably. Six core principles associated with social science research are set out that the ESRC expects to be addressed, whenever applicable:

- Research should be designed, reviewed and undertaken to ensure integrity and quality.
- Research staff and subjects must be informed fully about the purpose, methods and intended possible uses of the research, what their participation in the research entails and what risks, if any, are involved. Some variation is allowed in very specific and exceptional research contexts for which detailed guidance is provided in the policy guidelines.
- The confidentiality of information supplied by research subjects and the anonymity of respondents must be respected.
- Research participants must participate in a voluntary way, free from any coercion.
- Harm to research participants must be avoided.
- The independence of research must be clear, and any conflicts of interest or partiality must be explicit.

(ESRC 2005: 1)

Informed consent and gaining access to research settings are continuous processes. Try to demonstrate a continuous awareness of how you got around these issues throughout the research process. For example, don't just put a tiny ethics section in and forget about it: try to make it part of your overall research strategy.

Embedded within these principles are the commonly agreed international standards for good practice in research as laid down in the Declaration of Helsinki developed by the World Medical Association (WMA 2004), with the first version adopted in 1964 and including the following areas:

- beneficence (do positive good);
- non-malfeasance (do no harm);
- informed consent;
- confidentiality/anonymity.

The foundations of contemporary research ethics lie within medical research, and there are different research parameters in the social sciences to aspects of medical research. Many professional bodies such as the British Sociological Association, the American Sociological Association, the American Anthropological Association and the British Psychological Society have produced their own ethical codes. The emergence of internet-based research has resulted in a specialist code of ethics to support this work, produced by the Association of Internet Researchers (AOIR 2002).

> I used the British Sociological Association and Social Research Association guidelines that they make available online. Also, Alan Bryman's book *Social Research Methods* was great, particularly when I was feeling bogged down by all the various different things that had to be considered! His writing style was very user-friendly and made the whole thing seem less daunting.

The application of research ethics has historically focused upon self-regulation. However, in recent years, the emphasis has shifted towards external regulation, and, for first-time researchers, this means the choices you make about methods may need greater consideration of these contexts before you make decisions and proceed.

Research studies have to comply with all relevant legal requirements. This includes any data-protection legislation and appropriate screening of researchers working with vulnerable groups of people. This may mean undergoing a Criminal Records Bureau check, or its non-UK equivalent, and this will have a time and cost implication.

What does this mean for the design of my research project?

At the outset, you have to bear in mind that your overarching responsibility is to protect the rights and dignity of all your research participants. It is important, therefore, that alongside consideration of the efficacy of different data-collection methods you also understand their ethical implications and the subsequent time and workload associations. Any research that involves contact with human subjects will raise a number of questions, as Judith Pressle's quote illustrates.

> Finally, I offer some comments about what I think I have learned about ethics over the years. First, ethics at best are frameworks that guide decision making. They are not rules, regulations, or laws. Even ethicists who claim absolute values struggle with how those values apply in any given situation. What makes ethical decisions difficult is that several competing 'goods' may be at stake or several simultaneous 'bads' are to be avoided. I may arrive at an adequate answer, but it is rarely ideal. Second, a review of a research plan for protection of human participants provides only input from other researchers on

obvious problematic issues; it does not guarantee that the researcher will have no further ethical challenges. Third, feminist values of whatever kind provide us with ethical frameworks for our decision making, but we must still prioritize those values and decide how they are at play in any given situation.

(Pressle 2006: 516)

Working with 'vulnerable' research participants

One of the first questions you need to answer is whether your research may bring you into contact with participants who may be 'vulnerable' in a legal context. In law, 'vulnerable' has a particular meaning, but this will be dependent upon the legal jurisdiction in which you are conducting your research. In the UK, this differs across England and Wales, Scotland and Northern Ireland, and internationally there is even greater variation. Broadly, vulnerable participants may include the following:

- infants and children under a certain age (e.g. eighteen or sixteen);
- people with learning or communication difficulties;
- people in hospital or under the care of social services;
- people with mental illness, including those with addictions to drugs and alcohol;
- people who are elderly.

If you wish to recruit vulnerable participants who meet the criteria of the jurisdiction in which you are conducting your research, then you need to consider where and how you will be interacting with them.

Unsupervised contact may require you to undergo a screening or check to ensure you do not have a criminal record that would make contact inappropriate and unlawful, and this may take time and involve a cost to you. The school or institution where you are undertaking your research is likely to insist on this if you are having private unsupervised access to vulnerable research participants.

This does not mean that you cannot do research with these populations. It may be that you can arrange supervised access to them. For example, you may interact with children in a public place, such as the corner of a classroom, or in the presence of a teaching assistant, or in some other public venue within the institution, provided you are not alone with the participant. These are issues you need to consider at the design stage so you can formulate an appropriate methodology and timings to meet the constraints you may be facing.

Practicalities of addressing ethical issues

There are a range of issues related to research ethics and practical implications that you have to consider when designing your research project. These include:

- informed consent;
- protection of participants;
- debriefing;
- confidentiality;
- observational research;
- deception;
- withdrawal from the research;
- data storage.

Case study: will your dissertation need ethical approval?

Prior to conducting any research work, permission had been sought and approved by the university, the local authority and the Project Co-ordinator. However, I then discovered that the local Health Ethics Committee [UK] also needed to give approval. This meant destroying data from eight pilot interviews that I had already conducted. The approval process proved lengthy. An application form, letters of approval, study and interview protocols and other documentation had to be completed and sent off in triplicate.

Initially, permission was rejected due to concerns about the scientific quality of the project. The Ethics Committee queried:

- sampling issues;
- the process for obtaining informed consent from participants;
- the data-storage procedures;
- evidence of researcher's suitability to conduct the research;
- provisions to ensure personal safety while conducting the interviews;
- the exclusion criteria – in particular, gauging levels of intoxication of research participants.

As I found out – research is research – there are no concessions for students.

> After lengthy correspondence, it was agreed to remove questions regarding participants' medical history, which had only been included as 'icebreakers'. The interview schedule was changed, and the Ethics Committee standards were met. The process delayed the research by five months, time many students will not have.
>
> (Beverley Searle)

Informed consent

The notion of informed consent is very important. It refers to the need for research participants to have the right sort of information, at the right time, presented in an appropriate format to enable them to make a decision about whether to take part in a piece of research knowing the reasons and consequences. To facilitate informed consent, Wiles *et al.* (2005: 9) argue that, 'It is crucial that researchers understand the information needs of the group that they want to research and that they use this knowledge to provide information in a way that will enable potential study participants to understand what participation will involve.' All aspects of the research that are likely to affect their willingness to become participants should be disclosed. For research involving vulnerable participants, getting informed consent may involve briefing parents, teachers or carers about the study, who may act as gatekeepers.

The term 'informed consent' is in itself contested especially when thinking about children and adults with learning difficulties or mental impairments whose abilities to understand what is being asked of them cannot be assumed or measured easily. Again, aspects of this may be addressed in law. For example, in England, Gillick competence is used to enable children under sixteen years of age to self-consent to decision-making about things affecting their lives including research consent independent of parent/guardian consent. This notion has been picked up by other countries such as Australia. Even if children are able to give their own consent to participating in research, however, parents and guardians also need to be informed and to give their agreement as they will often control access to a child.

It is also imperative that participants understand that consent given at the start of a study may be withdrawn at any time should they change their mind and that they should have assurance that such withdrawal will have no negative consequences for them. For example, users of social care services may feel concerned that not participating in a study may affect access to service(s), and it should be made very clear to them that this would not be so. Bhattacharya (2007) discusses the process of gaining informed consent as a process of negotiation – but it is not one you are necessarily aiming to win. If, for example, a young person declines consent, this may be viewed as positive because the way consent was asked may have enabled them to say no rather than pressurizing them to say 'yes'.

You may wish to design an information sheet to brief potential participants about the study. If you are asking children for consent, you might want to use pictures and colour to engage their interest. A participant information sheet should be given before asking people to sign a consent form. An example of a consent form is also provided with the web resources provided for this book (www.routledge.com) but your institution may have a template that they wish you to use for your study, and you should check carefully which materials are available to you and which are a requisite.

For standard questionnaire studies, where the topic of the research is not a particularly sensitive issue, it may be sufficient to include a description of your study at the start of your questionnaire, completion of the questionnaire implying consent. Again, your supervisor will be able to advise you if you are uncertain.

Observational research

Unless the participants give their consent to being observed, observational research must only take place where those observed could normally expect to be observed by strangers.

Observational studies must not violate the individual's privacy and psychological well-being. You should also be sensitive to any cultural differences in definitions of public and private space.

Protection of participants

The Declaration of Helsinki, discussed earlier, provides the guiding principles here. As a researcher, you must take care at all times to protect your participants from physical and mental harm. If potentially distressing questions might be asked, participants must have the right not to answer these questions, and this must be made clear to them at the start. If negative consequences might ensue, then the researcher has to detect and remove these effects. This might, for example, involve having telephone numbers of helplines that participants could contact if they wanted to discuss the issues further. In research with children, you must not discuss the results you obtain from individual children with teachers and parents. In all cases, you can only report back your anonymized results unless you have child protection concerns.

Deception

In most social science research, deception should not be necessary. Sometimes, however, participants may modify their behaviour if they know what the researcher is looking for, so that by giving the full explanation to participants you cannot collect reliable data. Deception should only be used when no other method can be found for collecting reliable data and when the seriousness of the question justifies it. A distinction is made between deliberately deceiving participants and withholding of some information.

Deliberate deception is rarely justifiable. Withholding of information does occur more frequently. This might mean, for example, giving your questionnaire a general title such as 'An Exploration of Social Attitudes', rather than saying which attitudes in particular you are interested in. The guiding principle is taken to be the likely reaction of participants when the deception is revealed. If participants are likely to be angry or upset in some way, then deception should not occur. If any form of deception is involved, then you need to seek ethical approval for your study.

Debriefing

When deception has occurred, debriefing is particularly emphasized, but it should be a part of all research to monitor the experience of the participants for any unanticipated negative effects. This may involve providing participants with written information describing the study, the contact details of helplines or counselling services or health-care agencies that participants can contact if they wanted to discuss the issues further, or both. Participants should also know how to contact you after the study. Generally, the inclusion of your university email address is the best option, but there may be occasions when it is not appropriate to provide a means of having ongoing contact with you. Your supervisor will be able to advise you about this.

Withdrawal from the research

Sometimes individuals may get distressed during an interview, and you must make it clear that they can withdraw from the study at any time without giving any reason. It may be that a participant decides after an interview that they have said things that they now regret. Participants should be able to withdraw their interview data in cases such as this. It is good practice in your participant information sheet to give a cut-off date up to when participant data can be withdrawn. This will normally be up to the time when you intend to start your data analysis.

Confidentiality

Here you must conform to data-protection legislation, which means that information obtained from a research participant is confidential (unless you have agreed in advance that this is not to be the case). This means that you must take care to anonymize data that you obtain from participants, say in interview studies. To do this, you must not only change names but also change any details that might make the person easily identifiable. This should be done at the data-collation or transcription stage. You are required to assure your participants that this will occur.

Data storage

If you are collecting data from participants who are not anonymous, then you must take special precautions to ensure that the data is stored appropriately to ensure the participants' anonymity. This means that tapes should be kept securely, and they should not be labelled with participants' real names. You will have to keep your data sets until after you have passed your degree in case you are required to produce them by your university. Interview tapes and other confidential material should be disposed of carefully when no longer required.

Will my research need to be approved by a research ethics committee?

To some extent, this will depend on the arrangements within your own university; however, if your research involves patients, schoolchildren or users of social care services, then it is likely that your proposal will need to undergo special ethical review even if you think there are no particular ethical issues involved. The process involved will, of course, vary considerably between institutions and countries.

Guidelines for relatively standard research proposals

While it is not possible to provide definitive guidelines, scrutiny of these questions will help you decide whether your research proposal has special ethical issues that result in it requiring ethical review by your departmental/university research ethics committee or equivalent. Your supervisor will also provide you with further advice on this.

1   Does it involve human participants, or data from human participants? (Yes/No)

2   Does it involve vulnerable participants as defined below? (Yes/No)

- Infants and children under the age of eighteen?
- People with learning or communication difficulties?
- Patients in hospital or under the care of social services?
- People who are involved in the criminal-justice system (e.g. prisoners or those on probation orders)?
- People engaged in illegal activities such as drug abuse? (British Psychological Society 2004).

3   Does it involve sensitive topics (i.e. topics likely to cause significant embarrassment or discomfort to participants or topics related to illegal activity)? (Yes/No)

4   Does it involve collection of data that is not anonymous? (Yes/No)

If you have answered 'Yes' to Questions 2 and 3, you will normally be required to submit an ethics proforma for ethical approval by your departmental/university research ethics committee or equivalent. An example of a typical ethics proforma used for an undergraduate project is included on our supplementary web pages (www.routledge.com).

Guidelines for the special case when patient access is required for a research study

The National Health Service (NHS) in the UK has clearly defined the criteria for NHS research involving:

- patients and users of the NHS;
- relatives or carers of patients and users of the NHS;
- access to data, organs, or other bodily material of past and present NHS patients;
- foetal material and IVF involving NHS patients;
- the recently dead in NHS premises;
- the use of, or potential access to, NHS premises or facilities;
- NHS staff recruited as research participants by virtue of their professional role.

All projects with NHS involvement have to be presented for ethical review to an NHS research ethics committee. Full details of this process and forms for doing this can be accessed online at the NHS Patient Safety Agency's

National Research Ethics Service (www.nres.npsa.nhs.uk). Again, it is imperative to discuss this with your supervisor as you will need lots of time from the development of a firm proposal to obtaining the approval you need to proceed.

Being a responsible researcher

We have introduced you to the rules that govern ethical research, and now we want to shift the ground a bit towards the notion of being a responsible researcher. Clearly, meeting ethical requirements and conduct are part of this responsibility. However, we also want to mention other aspects of responsibility that are, it may be argued, more a question of personal morals and, to some extent, manners.

If you are involving others in your research, then you are inviting yourself into a part of their lives, asking something of people for which they will probably receive nothing in return. This raises the issue of offering some form of payment in exchange for participation. This is a contested area, and you may not be in a position to consider any kind of financial reward – for completing a questionnaire for example. However, you can show your appreciation by:

- being on time when you attend interviews;
- where possible, giving interview respondents the chance to look at and comment on their interview material in case they wish to change anything;
- thanking people afterwards in writing or by email;
- considering ways of disseminating your research to your participants if time and resources allow.

In some circumstances, you may wish to express your thanks to people who have been particularly helpful by small gifts such as chocolates to, for example, a community worker who has helped facilitate access to youth groups. Again, if you are unsure, ask your supervisor or fellow students for their views.

Responsibility in research also involves:

- doing justice to the data you have been able to collect;
- treating the data with integrity and not falsifying results;
- representing the views of participants in an authentic and respectful way;
- being aware of your personal biases in your treatment of data;
- engaging with others about your research and reflecting upon what you are doing, and how your actions may impact on others.

We do not wish to sound as though we are telling you what to do. However, we are aware that when we are busy and under pressure it can be tempting to let some things slip that are important, and doing research *does* carry responsibilities.

Key messages

- Morals are unwritten values used to distinguish the right from the wrong.
- Ethics are usually a written set of values which apply to a specific context.
- Codes of behaviour are used to protect the interests of research participants, since these interests are different and may even be at odds with those of the researcher.
- As a researcher, you must comply with the legal requirements binding your actions and the privacy of the research participants.
- Consult your supervisor and institutional procedures for guidance on gaining ethical approval for any study you are considering.
- Try to continuously reflect on what you are doing and check that your actions align with those of responsible researchers.

Key questions

- When I am conducting research, who is protecting the interests and rights of my subjects?
- Have I got a thorough checklist of tasks I need to do, with timelines attached?
- Have I kept my supervisor involved with discussions on research ethics?

Further reading

Francis, R. D. (1999) *A Code of Ethics for Psychologists*, Leicester: BPS Books.

Lee-Trewick, G. and Linkogle, S. (2000) *Danger in the Field: Risk and Ethics in Social Research*, London: Routledge.

Maunthner, M. and Birch, M. (2002) *Ethics in Qualitative Research*, London, Sage.

Pressle, J. (2006) 'Feminist Research Ethics', in S. Nagy Hesse-Bilber (ed.) *Handbook of Feminist Research*, London: Sage, pp. 515–534.

Walliman, N. (2005) *Your Research Project*, 2nd edn, London: Sage.

Chapter 8

Quantitative data analysis

Introduction

This chapter focuses on quantitative data analysis. It aims to give an overview of the ways in which you can analyse the data that you have spent so much time and energy collecting. The chapter is not intended to be a comprehensive guide to quantitative data analysis but an introduction to some of the options open to you. At the end of the chapter, there are recommended texts that will give you much more detail on the different techniques suggested here. You will carry out quantitative analysis if the data that you collect is numeric. If you have distributed questionnaires, conducted structured interviews or observations, or if you are doing analysis of existing survey data, you are likely to do quantitative analysis. All examples in this chapter are developed from the teaching data sets for the British Crime Survey 2000 and the British Health Survey 2002. These are available from the Data Archive (www.data-archive.ac.uk). All calculations were done using the quantitative data analysis package SPSS.

By the end of this chapter, you should have a better understanding of:

- how to prepare for your data analysis;
- the different types of variables;
- how to carry out univariate and bivariate analysis;
- the possibilities of multivariate analysis and inferential statistics;
- different software packages to help you analyse your data.

Preparing data for analysis

The first stage in quantitative data analysis is getting your data into a format that you can analyse. This usually involves creating a spreadsheet to put your data in (this could be in Excel or in a specialized software package

Table 8.1 Example of spreadsheet for data analysis

	Age	Gender	Ethnicity	Worry about burglary
01	67	1	4	2
02	23	2	8	2
03	44	1	1	4

such as SPSS). As you design your file, you should ensure that each column represents a variable and each row represents a case (see Table 8.1). A case is usually a person (but could also be a city, an organization, a country, etc.); a variable is an attribute on which cases vary (for example ethnicity) (Bryman 2004: 29). If you have lots of questions and a large sample, you will have a very large spreadsheet.

Since it is easier to analyse numeric data than a mixture of characters and letters (Bryman and Cramer 1990: 19), you should aim to code all your data numerically. When you ask your respondent to complete your questionnaire, you usually ask them to choose from a category that you have already given a number (pre-coding); for example: in a question about transport, option 1 could represent 'bus', option 2 'train', option 3 'car', etc. Respondents might also be asked to give a number (their age or weight). Alternatively, you may have open questions in your questionnaire that need to be post-coded. This is where you assign the codes after you have collected the data. These codes could be based on themes that you have found in your questionnaire data or in the literature you have read. Sometimes you might want to recode your data. You might decide it is more practical to have age in age brackets (21–30; 31–40; etc.) rather than using the exact age of your respondents in your analysis. You also need to assign a number to missing values. So, if someone does not answer a question, you need to have some way of representing that. If your codes from ethnicity run through 1 to 9; then 99 could represent missing data because it's out of your variable range. The important points when assigning your codes are (Bryman 2004: 146):

1   There must be no overlap of categories (that is when one code is used for more than one category).
2   The list of categories must accommodate all possibilities (including missing data).
3   There needs to be rules about how codes are applied. This is to make sure that codes are applied consistently.

When you have finished coding and inputting data into your spreadsheet, you will have a dataset which is ready to analyse. However, before you get down to the analysis, you need to think about the kinds of data you are working with.

The quality of the data and design are more important than the complexity of the analysis (Gorard 2003: 230).

Variables

Not all numeric data are the same. An understanding of the differences between variables is important when choosing which calculations to do with your data. There are three main types of variable.

1 *Nominal.* This is when numbers are used like names. In a questionnaire, for example, certain questions might be coded with numbers to represent different categories. In a question on country of birth, Afghanistan might be coded as 1, Albania as 2, Algeria as 3, etc. The numbers 1, 2 and 3 have no numeric value and have been chosen arbitrarily. We could easily have chosen to code Albania as 9 and Algeria as 11. These categories cannot be rank ordered, and it would be meaningless to carry out certain statistical tests (such as calculating the mean) on nominal data. Other examples of nominal data include ethnicity, eye colour and housing tenure.

2 *Ordinal.* For these variables, the numbers represent categories again, but this time they can be rank ordered through the use of Likert-type scales. For example, levels of satisfaction can be numbered from 1 to 5, where 1 = extremely satisfied, 2 = satisfied, 3 = neither satisfied nor not satisfied, 4 = not satisfied, 5 = not satisfied at all. With these kinds of data it is possible to describe people's level of satisfaction, e.g. 'Sixty-seven per cent of respondents were very satisfied with the service.' It is important to remember, however, that the distances across the categories might not be equal. The researcher cannot judge whether someone who gives a 5 for satisfaction is five times less satisfied than someone who gives a 1. This means that, as with nominal data, certain calculations, such as mean and standard deviation, cannot be carried out on ordinal data. Other examples of ordinal data include: age categories (21–30, 31–40, etc.) or frequency of doing something (never, rarely, often, frequently).

3 *Interval/Ratio.* Here, the differences between the numbers are equal across the range. If someone is twenty-one and someone else is eighteen, the difference is three years. These three years are equal to the three-year difference between someone who is thirty-five and someone else who is thirty-two. The distinction between interval and ratio data is that the zero in interval data is arbitrary. For example, on

a thermometer, the zero for Fahrenheit and Celsius scales is different. In social science research, most variables will have a fixed zero – so they are *ratio* variables. It is possible to carry out more complex calculations and statistical tests on interval and ratio data. Examples of ratio data include age, income, height or weight.

Think about your data and decide which types of variables you are working with.

Descriptive analysis

The volume of numbers from which you need to create order and meaning can be intimidating at the start of data analysis. You need to find ways to summarize the data so that you can more easily see what the data is telling you. As you describe and summarize your data, you will be making it more readable, comprehensible and clear. Here we will look at how you can describe one variable and then compare two variables.

Univariate analysis

In univariate analysis, you are dealing with only one variable. You are not looking for differences between variables but are looking to describe the distribution of a variable. Through univariate analysis, you will describe tendencies, trends and patterns.

Frequency distributions

One way of presenting your data is through frequency distributions. This will show the number of people and the percentage for each category in your variable.

Frequency distributions can be used for all types of variable (nominal, ordinal, interval/ratio) mentioned above. The way you present your frequency distribution will depend on the variables you are describing. You can present your data in tables or graphs (pie-charts, bar charts, histograms). A good rule of thumb is to use a table unless a graph can put across the message more clearly. Table 8.2 shows a frequency table for the ethnicity of respondents in the British Crime Survey. Ethnicity is a nominal variable. People identifying themselves as 'White' make up the biggest percentage in this dataset at 97 per cent.

Frequency tables are also useful with ordinal data. Table 8.3 shows the results for the question 'How worried are you about being mugged or

Table 8.2 Frequency of ethnicities in the British Crime Survey

	Frequency	Percentage
White	18,345	97
Black	264	1
Asian	405	2
Total	19,014	100

Table 8.3 Frequency of worry of being robbed or mugged (British Crime Survey)

	Frequency	Percent
Very worried	3,272	17
Fairly worried	5,133	27
Not very worried	8,090	42
Not at all worried	2,827	15
Total	19,222	100

robbed?' The respondents were able to choose 'very worried', 'fairly worried', 'not very worried' and 'not at all worried'.

Table 8.3 shows that in this sample, most people are 'not very worried' about being mugged or robbed (42 per cent).

Interval data is a category of data which is often best represented graphically, through a histogram.

Figure 8.1 has a positive skew. The respondents tend to cluster to the left in a long tail towards the person who ate the most fruit and vegetables in twenty-four hours (twenty-seven portions!).

When you present the frequencies of your variables, take time to ensure that you are using the clearest presentation to describe that data.

Measures of central tendency

The measure of central tendency is a single figure that best represents the distribution of values in your data set. What we are looking for here is the average value. There are three forms of average.

The most commonly used one in everyday life is the 'mean'. It is the sum of all observations divided by number of observations. In this example, thirteen people were asked how many times their car had been stolen over the last year. They gave the following responses:

$$0 + 5 + 1 + 8 + 0 + 0 + 2 + 9 + 3 + 1 + 0 + 2 + 1$$

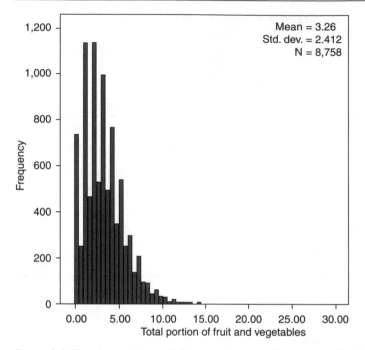

Figure 8.1 Total portions of fruit and vegetables eaten in 24-hour period (British Health Survey).

If you add these responses together, you get 32.

The mean = sum of observations/*n* (number)

The sum of observations is 32, and this is divided by the number of respondents, 13: 32/13. The mean for this study is = 2.5. The mean should only be used with interval data.

The 'median' is the score that occurs in the middle of the distribution of scores when they are displayed from smallest to largest. Continuing the example above, the numbers of times the car has been stolen can be arranged from the least to the most:

0, 0, 0, 0, 1, 1, 1, 2, 2, 3, 5, 8, 9

The median is the midpoint. To find which number is the midpoint, you use the following equation: (*n* + 1)/2. The number of respondents here was 13. So: 13 + 1 = 14/2 = 7. The median score is the 7th value, or 1. The median can be used with *interval data* (as in this example) or with *ordinal data* (where each number represents a category, but the order is important).

The third kind of average is the 'mode'. The mode is the most frequently occurring value in the distribution. In our example, the mode would be 0 as it occurs four times. The mode can be used for all types of variable. For nominal data, the mode is the only measure of central tendency that can be used.

Measures of spread

The measure of spread can tell you how dispersed your data is. In a study, a small spread is a good thing. It shows that there is little variance in the results so the mean represents the data well. If there is a large spread of results, then the mean will not be representative. There are different ways of calculating spread.

The 'range' is the difference between the highest and the lowest score. In our example, the least number of times that a car was stolen was 0 and the most was 9. This gives us a range of 9. You could use the range to compare two groups of people in different cities to see which group had more variability. It is, however, quite limited in what it can tell you.

If you calculate 'quartiles', you can gain more detailed information about the shape of the distribution. As with the median, the ordered data is divided up. Here it is divided into four. In our example, we already know the second quartile as this is the median − 1. The first quartile is between the third (0) and fourth (0) value, so is 0. The third quartile is between the tenth (3) and eleventh (5) value, so is 4. The 'interquartile range' is the difference between the first and the third quartiles: $4 - 0 = 4$. The interquartile range is seen as more robust than the range because it is less affected by outliers (those values which are significantly higher or significantly lower than the rest of the sample).

You can also work out how much a result deviates from the mean. 'Standard deviation' is the average amount of variation around the mean. To calculate the standard deviation, you need to divide the sum of squares by the number of values in your data set and then take the square root of that number. A worked example might help here:

Using the values from our example, we can work out the deviation of each value from the mean (the mean is 2.5). The results are shown in Table 8.4.

The sum of squares (111.25) is then divided by the number of values (13). This gives a variance of 8.6. This figure is then square-rooted to give

Table 8.4 Sum of squares

Value	Deviation (score − mean)	Squared deviation
0	−2.5	6.25
0	−2.5	6.25
0	−2.5	6.25
0	−2.5	6.25
1	−1.5	2.25
1	−1.5	2.25
1	−1.5	2.25
2	−0.5	0.25
2	−0.5	0.25
3	0.5	0.25
5	2.5	6.25
8	5.5	30.25
9	6.5	42.25
Sum of square		111.25

the standard deviation (2.9). The smaller the standard deviation, the more concentrated the values are around the mean. The less variance in the values, the less difference between the people in the sample (meaning your result will be more representative).

Don't worry if the sums here look a little complicated – there are computer packages that can help with these calculations! These are introduced at the end of this chapter.

To recap, to describe one variable, you can summarize

• the frequency of categories in a variable;
• the frequencies of distribution by calculating the average (mean, median and mode);
• the spread of the distribution (range, interquartile range and the standard deviation).

Table 8.5 gives the techniques for summarizing single variables.

Bivariate analysis

Whereas with univariate analysis the focus was on a description of one variable, here we are looking at the relationships between two variables: the explanatory and the outcome variable. The explanatory variable is the variable which is thought to be the variable of influence (it is also known as the independent, input or predictor variable). The outcome variable

Table 8.5 Techniques for univariate description

Variable	Numerical	Average	Spread
Nominal	Frequency table	Mode	Proportion in mode category
Ordinal	Frequency table	Median Mode	Interquartile range
Interval/Ratio		Mean Median	Standard deviation

(also known as the dependent variable) is the one that we believe will be affected by the explanatory variable.

For bivariate analysis, you need to remember the types of variable discussed in the last section. When you know which variables you are dealing with, you can employ the most appropriate techniques.

Remember that nominal and ordinal data were used to describe data that could be categorized (the difference being that ordinal data can be rank ordered). As a result of this, both nominal and ordinal data are termed: *categorical*. Interval and ratio data can also be called *scale* or *continuous* data, since it is possible to position both interval and scale data on a continuous scale. Using categorical and continuous headings as a starting point, it is possible to identify four bivariate scenarios. These scenarios are shown in Table 8.6.

We will look at each one in turn.

Categorical explanatory variable and categorical outcome variable

If you examine the relationship between two categorical variables, you are likely to carry out a cross-tabulation and present your analysis as a contingency table. A contingency table resembles a frequency table, but, rather than examining one variable, you are looking at two. A contingency table is the simplest and the most frequently used method for 'demonstrating the presence or absence of a relationship' between variables (Bryman and

Table 8.6 Bivariate scenarios

	Explanatory/independent variable	Outcome/dependent variable
1	Categorical	Categorical
2	Categorical	Continuous
3	Continuous	Continuous
4	Continuous	Categorical

Table 8.7 Contingency table for 'worry about being mugged or robbed' and 'gender' (British Crime Survey)

Worry about being mugged/ robbed	Gender		Total (%)
	Female (%)	Male (%)	
Very worried	2,382 (23)	882 (10)	3,272 (17)
Fairly worried	3,230 (31)	1,903 (22)	5,133 (27)
Not very worried	3,930 (37)	4,160 (47)	8,090 (42)
Not at all worried	971 (9)	1,856 (21)	2,827 (15)
TOTAL	10,520 (100)	8,802 (100)	19,322 (100)

Cramer 1990: 151). It is common for the presumed independent variable to be the column variable and the presumed dependent variable to be the one in the row (Bryman 2004: 231).

The two variables under analysis in Table 8.7 are 'worry about being mugged or robbed' and 'gender'.

The column variable is 'Gender'. This is presumed to be the influencing variable. The row variable is 'Worry about being mugged or robbed'; this is the variable that we presume to be influenced. So, in this example, we believe that gender might well be an influencing factor in terms of how worried you are about crime.\When interpreting the result of your test, you need to focus on the percentages rather than the counts in each cell. The percentages are column percentages. That means that the number in a cell is a percentage of the total in that column. In this example, women are more likely to be very worried about being mugged/robbed than men (23 per cent as opposed to 10 per cent). Men are also more likely to not be worried at all (21 per cent) than women (9 per cent). This seems to suggest that women are generally more worried about being mugged or robbed than men. Adding the column totals for 'very worried' and 'fairly worried' provides more evidence for this. Fifty-four per cent of women and 32 per cent of men are worried about being mugged and robbed.

Categorical explanatory variable and continuous outcome variable

Here your independent variable is categorical (e.g. social class, job satisfaction) and the dependent variable is scale (e.g. income or annual leave). In order to compare these two variables, you will carry out a comparison of means. The mean of the scale variables will be compared with each subgroup in your categorical variable. We might, for example, think that

Table 8.8 Comparison of means for 'portions of fruit and vegetables eaten' and 'gender' (British Health Survey)

	Mean	Number	Standard deviation	Median	Minimum	Maximum
Male	3.1	4,000	2.4	2.7	0	24
Female	3.4	4,758	2.4	3.0	0	27
Total	3.3	8,758	2.4	3.0	0	27

women are likely to eat more fruit and vegetables than men. We can run a comparison of means to test this. The results are shown in Table 8.8.

The table shows that there is little difference between men and women's fruit and vegetable consumption, although women do appear to eat slightly more on average. To test whether that difference was significant, you would have to run further tests.

The output can also be shown in a box plot as in Figure 8.2. The box plot shows us the distribution of the data more clearly than in Table 8.8.

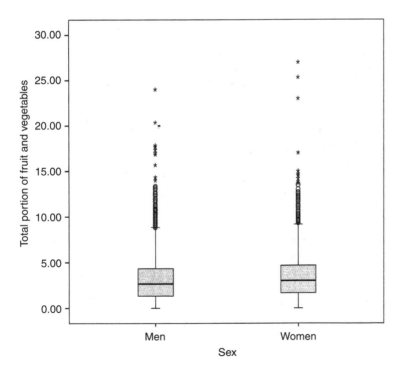

Figure 8.2 Box plot for 'portions of fruit and vegetables eaten' and 'gender' (British Health Survey).

The box plot shows all of the following: the smallest observation (the bottom horizontal line), the bottom 25 per cent (the section between the lowest observation and the grey box), the interquartile range (the grey box), the mean (thick black line), the top 25 per cent (section above the grey box) and the highest observation (upper horizontal line). The box plot shows whether this is a symmetrical or skewed distribution. In this example, it is skewed: there is more spread for both men and women in the upper 25 per cent. You cannot see this spread in the same way in Table 8.8.

The box plot also indicates where there might be outliers. Outliers are cases which are very different from the rest of the cases. They are shown here by circles and stars. Sometimes outliers are the result of someone having inputted the data incorrectly, so you may remove them. However, you need to think carefully before excluding data from your analysis. In this example, you need to be convinced that people were not capable of eating ten or more (up to twenty-seven) portions of fruit and vegetables in one twenty-four-hour period.

Continuous explanatory variable and continuous outcome variable

Here both variables are continuous. You could, for example, be examining the relationship between income and GCSE ('General Certificate of Secondary Education' is the name of a set of educational qualifications taken by students in England, Wales and Northern Ireland), point score or height and weight. The scatter plot is the best way to look at the relationship between two continuous variables.

In Figure 8.3, there is a positive relationship between the two variables. The cluster is linear and is moving upward towards the right. This means that the taller people were the more likely to weigh more. Intuitively, this makes sense. You can also have negative relations. Here, as one variable increases, the other would decrease. If there was no relationship between the variables, there would be no clear pattern in the plots. Figure 8.3 suggests that there is a relationship between these two variables. It is not saying that one variable causes another to increase. To identify causation, you would have to carry out more complex statistical tests.

Measuring correlation

You can carry out calculations to assess to what extent your two variables are related. The results of your calculations are called 'correlation coefficients',

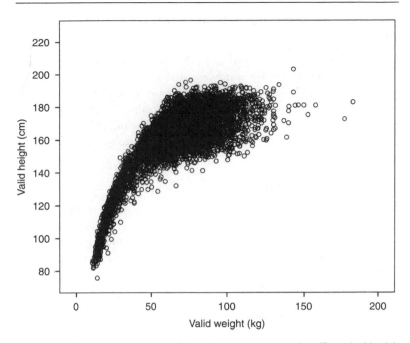

Figure 8.3 Scatter diagram of height against weight (British Health Survey).

and they are usually a value between 0 and 1. Here are two common correlation coefficients:

* *Pearson's r.* This measures the relationship between two continuous variables. The value ranges from −1 (a perfect negative relationship) through 0 (no relationship) to +1 (perfect positive relationship). In order to conduct a Pearson's r test, your data needs to meet certain assumptions: the two variables need to have a normal distribution (i.e. the histogram would look like an upside-down bell) and then when plotted on a scatter plot there needs to be a linear relationship between them.

* *Spearman's rho.* This test is similar to Pearson's r but your data do not need to meet the same assumptions. In this test, variables are ranked. A ranking of +1 shows a perfect relationship. It is possible to use Spearman's rho with both continuous and categorical data.

Continuous explanatory variable and categorical outcome variable

It is very rare to come across this scenario. If you do, consider categorizing your continuous variable (for example, putting ages into age brackets) and then using the techniques such as contingency tables or following the techniques above but paying close attention to the interpretation. There are more advanced approaches to deal with this situation, but they are beyond the scope of this book and most undergraduate work.

Multivariate analysis

You can analyse more than two variables simultaneously, and this is called 'multivariate analysis'. The techniques used to do this kind of analysis are quite advanced, so if you are keen to do this you need to be working with a book that deals specifically with quantitative analysis (see recommended reading list).

Beyond descriptive analysis to inferential statistics

Using descriptive analysis, you will have described the data that you have collected and identified relationships between those variables. The next stage in analysis is to test to what extent the results of the data in your sample are generalizable to your sample's population. These tests are called hypothesis tests or tests for statistical significance. The results from these tests tell you how confident you can be that the relationships observed in the sample are representative of that population. You would use different hypothesis tests depending on the types of variables you are analysing (for example, categorical explanatory and outcome variables would require a chi-square test of association, then Phi or Cramer's V). All of these tests will carry with them certain assumptions about your data. For example, they might require that your data be normally distributed, independent, continuous. However, in terms of hypothesis-testing there is one assumption that is extremely important. The data needs to have been drawn from a random sample. Hypothesis tests are carried out when you want to know whether something found is a quirk of the data set or something that is a feature of the population. A test carried out on a non-random sample cannot speak with confidence about generalizing to the population. If your sample is not random, you would be advised to spend your time carrying out a thorough descriptive analysis and trying to interpret what is happening in the sample that you have collected. If you collect your own data for your undergraduate dissertation, you are unlikely to have a truly random sample large enough to analyse with inferential statistics. For this reason, we will not go into any more detail about inferential statistics here. If you are working with a random sample (if you're analysing data that has been collected by someone else as part of a much bigger survey, for example), look at some of the books in the list at the end of this chapter that will introduce you to some of the more sophisticated statistical techniques. Also, discuss analysis options with your dissertation supervisor.

Data interpretation

The techniques described above offer you ways to summarize, describe and compare your data. Importantly, however, you will also need to interpret that data by asking yourself what is the data trying to tell you. You should return to your initial hypothesis, research question or theory and see whether your data supports them. You need to explain why the data are saying what they are saying. In order to do this, you will need to draw on your knowledge of the topic area (gained from your reading) and also your reflection on your research approach. (For example, were there limitations to your study that may have resulted in certain findings.) Your interpretation should show how your research has extended, confirmed or confounded understandings of the social world.

A tip regarding data analysis would be not to attempt to analyse too much data. Pick a shorter time span, a smaller population or maybe fewer indices. Using up a lot of time on data analysis is not always productive.

Using software to analyse data

Do not despair if you have read through this chapter so far and wondered how on earth you would be able to do all of these calculations and produce the complicated tables and graphs – there is software to help you!

The most commonly used statistics package designed originally for social scientists is SPSS. It is relatively easy to use, and there are many good books that will introduce you to the functions that you will need for your dissertation (SPSS is a powerful piece of software which has functionality way beyond what you will need for your research). Your institution might well have a licence for SPSS. There are many online guides, textbooks and chapters in data-analysis books that will introduce you step-by-step to SPSS. Take a look at these texts and work through some of the examples before you start to analyse your own data.

There are other packages available, some of which are free access – for example Openstat. And don't forget Excel in the Microsoft Office package. The statistics functionality is good, and freely available add-ons can give more advanced features.

These programs will be able to do the calculations mentioned here and will produce graphs, plots and tables to present the data. The computer package, however, only works with what you input. That is why this chapter has concentrated more on what the different techniques show rather than demonstrating how you carry them out in different packages. It is really important, then, that you understand the tests you are asking the software to do. If not, you might find that when you present your findings that they are meaningless.

Key messages

- You need to understand the data that you are working with so that any calculations that you perform are valid.
- Descriptive analysis allows you to examine the variables you have in your data set and to establish relationships between them.
- There is no point conducting tests to establish the generalizability of your findings if you have a small sample, collected through convenience sampling.
- If you are carrying out analysis of an existing data set, techniques of inferential statistics might well be appropriate.
- Investigate computer packages that will help you with your analysis – investment of time in learning the software will pay dividends in terms of time spent analysing the data.

Key questions

- Does your university support a data-analysis package? Have you identified a package that can help you?
- Do you know which variables you are working with?
- Have you described your data using the appropriate techniques?
- Have you used the right checks to establish relationships between your variables?
- Does your sample comply with the assumptions necessary to carry out tests of statistical significance?
- Have you allowed enough time to interpret your statistics?

Further reading

Bryman, A. (2004) *Social Research Methods*, 2nd edn, Oxford: Oxford University Press.

Bryman, A. and Cramer, D. (2005) *Quantitative Data Analysis with SPSS 12 and 13. A Guide for Social Scientists*, London: Routledge.

Field, A. (2005) *Discovering Statistics Using SPSS*, London: Sage.

Gorard, S. (2003) *Quantitative Methods in the Social Science: The Role of Numbers Made Easy*, London: Continuum.

Chapter 9

Qualitative data analysis

Introduction

In the last chapter we focused on how to analyse numeric data. Here, we turn to the analysis of talk, text and visual data. These data include written, printed or web texts, transcripts of spoken language, field notes from observations, research memos and also images (Fairclough 2003: 3). Just as the data sources are wide ranging, so too are the strategies by which these data can be analysed. There is no singularly correct way to carry out qualitative data analysis. Qualitative data analysis is time-consuming, interpretative and iterative; it involves close attention to detail and good organizational skills. As highlighted in Chapter 8, to properly analyse data, you need to allocate sufficient time and resources when you plan your project.

By the end of this chapter, you should have a better understanding of:

- preparing your data for analysis;
- the phases of qualitative data analysis;
- software packages to aid data analysis;
- specific approaches to qualitative data analysis;
- how to assess the quality of your data analysis.

Preparing data for analysis

You might be lucky enough to have data in a form which is ready to analyse, for example, documents in an electronic form that you can manipulate. You are likely, however, to have written notes, audio files and visual data. Researchers usually prefer to have a neatly typed textual copy to work with (Gibbs 2007: 7); the process to get there is called transcription. You can carry out transcription with different levels of detail. Sometimes a

46	I	So what kind of things do they need then, this group particularly?
47	R	Well, I think, um, in terms (…) uh, th-the /?/ it's partly an issue you know, kind
48		of about what we set up for them in terms of the teaching. So if we—
49	I	Yeah.
50	R	…/educationally/, I mean so much of our teaching to data has been geared
51		toward maturer applicants who maybe have more experience of the practice of
52		social work. So we're having to think more actively about, about how to, to
53		manage our teaching so that it copes, it is appropriate to both groups of
54		students.
55	I	Right, yeah.
56	R	Um…er, you know, so that we're not completely talking over the heads of the
57		new students in terms of these, and the kind of historical things that we're
58		talking about, let alone the kind of intellectual ones.
59	I	Yeah, yeah.
60	R	Um, so so there's that. For those students, I, and yeah, I suppose in that
61		regard you know, one of the things that, which is not exactly answering your
62		que-, not directly answering your question, but it's sort of indicative of what
63		we've identified /as needs/, is that within the last, within this last year we have
64		specifically developed a, um, a special set of activities, really, opportunities for
65		those groups of students to go and just explore—
66	I	Right.
67	R	…different social work and social care agencies, you know, over and above the
68		opportunities that students would ordin-, ordinarily have. You know, because
69		that helps give them a bit more grounding in what's being talked about.
70	I	Yeah.
71	R	So that's the academics, you know, the subject support thing.
72	I	Yeah.
73	R	Um, I think that um socially um you know those students, h- um (…) you know
74		ther-, as I say, you know, kind of numbers on board living away from home for
75		the first time, there's, there's not a lot, that won't be true for all of them, you
76		know, but um, and dealing with the social challenges of living in halls, which has
77		you know pros and cons to it, I suppose. You can feel very isolated as well as
78		very together with people in those kinds of settings I think.
79	I	Yeah, yeah.

Figure 9.1 Extract from a verbatim transcript.

transcription that just captures the gist is okay, common in policy research (Gibbs 2007: 13). The most commonly used approach is verbatim. This is where you note who said what and what they said. It is important that you remove any identifying features from the transcripts (such as names). Figure 9.1 shows an extract from a verbatim transcript.

In your transcription, you might tidy up the language so that all the conversational fillers such as 'erm' are removed, but equally you might leave them in. If you are doing conversational or discourse analysis, you are probably going to want to have more detail in your transcript, including markers of stress, intonation and changes in pitch or volume. There are transcription guidelines to help you; Silverman (2000: 298–299) or Rapley

(2007: 57–60) offer some examples. If working with video-based data, you need to bear other things in mind as well such as: gaze, touch, gesture, spatial positioning and other actions (Rapley 2007: 54–55). Transcription is time-consuming. It is estimated that for each hour of recording, it takes four to six hours to transcribe (Gibbs 2007: 10). The more detailed your recording, the longer it will take. You need to make sure you have planned for this time.

Whenever you do a transcription, you have to remember that it will always only be partial and selective (Rapley 2007: 70). This is because transcription involves changing the medium which raises questions about 'accuracy, fidelity and interpretation' (Gibbs 2007: 11). At the very least, you should check your transcription against the original. Although it seems like a long and tedious task, transcribing your own data gives you a head start with your data analysis because you will become very familiar with it.

Phases in qualitative data analysis

In an article written for 'rookie' qualitative researchers, Baptiste (2001) outlines a framework which aims to help researchers new to qualitative data analysis see the common features of qualitative data analysis. The paper was written because he found that his students were bewildered by the multitude of approaches to qualitative data analysis. He outlines four phases:

1   defining the analysis;
2   classifying the data;
3   making connections between and among categories of data;
4   conveying the message or the write-up (see Figure 9.2).

This last phase is covered in Chapter 10. Here we'll concentrate on only the first three.

Defining the analysis

This first phase is as much a part of your research design as it is a part of data analysis, further highlighting the point that design, data collection and data analysis are inextricably linked – especially in qualitative research.

The approach adopted for data analysis is often dependent on what you consider to be valued as knowledge: your epistemology. The epistemological questions that you ask yourself relate to how you would try to

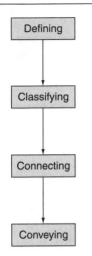

Figure 9.2 Phases in qualitative data analysis.

acquire knowledge, what you believe counts as knowledge and how you would know (Baptiste 2001). You should also consider what you deem to be real: your ontology. When we think about ontological positions, we need to be clear about what we see as real and how our understanding of reality shapes how we do our research (Baptiste 2001). A further consideration is around the values and ethics associated with your approach to your research: your axiology. You need to consider to what extent your values will impact on your analysis, the role that your research participants will play in your research and what you will then do with the output of your research.

It may seem that this section is encouraging you to ask some very hard and deeply philosophical questions about your research: that is the aim. Qualitative analysis is interpretive, and your epistemological, ontological and axiological positions will inevitably influence your methodology and subsequently your approach to analysis. It is therefore important for you to be able to articulate your position and to be able to evaluate the impact that position will have on your research – particularly its strengths and limitations.

Classifying the data

In Phase 2, you begin the process of classifying your data. Becoming familiar with that data is one of your first priorities. Before you formally begin your analysis, you should allocate some time to briefly look through and read the data collected. This will include listening to the tapes of any interviews and reading through the transcripts, looking at the notes you wrote for yourself during the data-collection period, and watching any video footage that you have. As you go through this cycle of reading and rereading, you will already be starting to notice patterns and similarities in your data. You are beginning to develop a template for conducting the full analysis.

> Analysis was massively time-consuming, because I kept wanting to go back over transcripts when new ideas occurred to me – so make sure you leave enough time to do that! And the best tip I had from a member of staff was that analysis isn't about reporting what your participants say – it's about what they mean, taking the step up from just describing to actually understanding their views.

In the next stage, you will start to further develop the template through coding. The process of coding involves picking out the bits of your data set that you think are interesting and useful for the research that you are carrying out. As you continue with your analysis, you may find that the notes you are making can be developed into codes or labels. The same codes might come up frequently; so, you can then read through the data set and highlight every time that the code is represented. These codes are emergent from your data, and your analysis is inductive. You can choose to use the actual words that are used in your data set as your labels – this is called 'in-vivo coding' – or you can choose to name them yourself.

It is also possible to analyse your data more deductively. Here, the template is given and not emergent, meaning that you go into the data set looking for specific concepts which you allocate codes before you start your analysis. These concepts will most likely be based on or drawn from the literature you have read.

You may even decide to combine both inductive and deductive coding. You might begin to look through your data sets for specific codes (deductive approach) but also make note of any emergent or unexpected codes (inductive). Whichever approach you choose will be dependent on how you defined your analysis in Phase 1.

There are different ways that you can mark your codes. You may choose to make notes of key words in the margin of your transcript. You might prefer to get out your highlighter pens and to mark up the codes in different colours. You will find that some pieces of data will relate to more than

```
 1  (I) But you did alright didn't you? You got a good mark
 2  (R) Yeah yeah
 3  (I) Yeah? So what do you think? I mean you got a 2:1 and you say you just, you
 4  know, just did enough. Yet what strategies did you use then in order to get that I mean
 5  cos you could easily have got a 2:2 couldn't you, with that?
 6  (R) Yeah
 7  (I) Approach but you got a 2:1. What do you think you learned, in terms of working in
 8  academia that got you the 2:1 and not a 2:2?
 9  (R) Basically I knew how to like balance my life, like the social aspect of it,
10  and I knew when to study           Strategy
11  (I) OK, so you could, like, if you had an exam coming up you would-
12  (R) Yeah definitely. And when I was studying my undergrad I was like so far away
13  from home and I was thinking well I've come all this way I don't want to go home,
14  you know, disappointing my family, cos what was the point in me going all this way
15  if I was going to go home and fail.
16  (I) Yep                                                    Worried him
17  (R) So that was always playing at the back of my mind
18  (I) Ok so there was that pushing you, yep, ok. So coming into this course then. Do you
19  think that there are any particular skills that you needed in order to do well on this
20  module?
21  (R) I think like the past four years I've lacked in confidence, so one of the reasons was
22  to gain in confidence cos I just felt you know I was you know like useless in life cos
23  I'd not like made really much use out of my first degree
24  (I) Yep                                                ~ Build person
25  (R) So I just come here to like build up my confidence, mainly
26  (I) Yep. Do you think that this module has helped you do that?
27  (R) Yes but I feel as though I didn't help myself by participating more in group work
28  (I)Ok.
                            Not pushed himself
```

Figure 9.3 **Example of a coded extract.**

one code, so you need to be sure that the method you have adopted can cater for these overlaps. The important point is that you find a method that works for you. Figure 9.3 shows a transcript which is in the process of being annotated.

As you work through the data identifying codes and highlighting them, you may begin to suffer from 'code overload'. At this point, you need to stand back and see whether you are using different codes to describe the same thing. If you are, then you should see whether only one code can be used instead. This type of pruning the codes used throughout analysis will be ongoing.

Having coded all of your data, you can now start to look for ways to connect those codes together into themes, concepts or categories. As you do this, you should be checking whether these themes are distinct from each other and that you have sufficient data to support each of them. You should be willing to redefine the categories as you go deeper into your analysis.

In order to do this grouping, you may decide to cut up a printed version of your transcripts and cluster your codes together into different categories. The beauty of this approach is that you can keep moving the pieces around until you find the most suitable home for them. You could use the cut and paste function in your word-processing package to copy fragments of your data into a document named after the theme. When you do this, keep the contextual detail of your extracts (e.g. which transcript or which set of field notes the data came from). It is important that you can reference where your materials come from. If you are systematic here, it will save you a lot of time later down the line. If not, time will be wasted searching for individual quotes. You might, for example, choose to display your categories diagrammatically through concept maps (see Chapter 4) or spider diagrams, as in Figure 9.4. As with coding, you need to find a

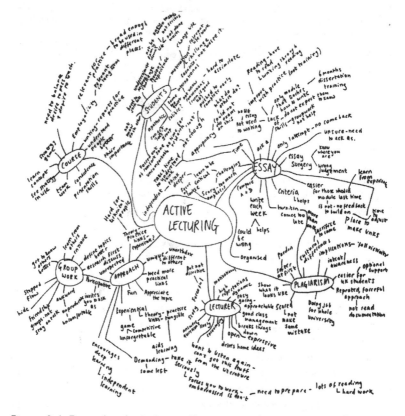

Figure 9.4 Example of mind map (for you to view, not to read).

method which allows you to see the connections between your data more clearly.

The process described should not be seen as linear but as iterative. You enter a 'messy' cycle of coding, defining and refining (Baptiste 2001). It is important to remember that coding is not the totality of data analysis; it is only a part of it (Bryman 2004: 409). Coding allows you to reduce and synthesize your data set so that you are able to deal with what often appears to be an insurmountable mass of data. Codes are argued to 'empower and speed up analysis' (Miles and Huberman 1994: 65), although it is worth remembering that coding is time-consuming and tiring – so, pace yourself. Miles and Huberman (1994: 65) suggest that combining coding with other activities (writing memos or reflective comments, for example) so that the brain does not become dull to the classification process. If not, regular breaks from lengthy periods of coding are recommended.

Following classification, data analysis becomes more creative and more interesting. You need to see what the categories created mean to the people involved in the research and how they relate to your research questions and the research literature in your chosen area (Bryman 2004: 409). At this stage, you enter the third phase: making connections.

Making connections

In this phase, the aim is to help you and your readers to understand more deeply and more broadly the area investigated. Baptiste (2001) uses the ideas of story development and theory building to explain this process. In the previous phase, 'classifying the data' was used to help display, in a different way, what the data was telling you. The point of research, however, is not to repeat what is already known, neither is it to act as 'a mere mouthpiece' (Bryman 2004: 411) for your interviewees. Research is about interpreting and theorizing data, and in doing so you gain understanding.

These interpretations then need to be made public and be opened for critique by your dissertation supervisor, external examiners, peers, the research stakeholders and possibly a wider audience (if you try to publish – see Chapter 12). To survive such scrutiny, you need to have confidence in your analysis.

As you interpret your findings, you will be looking for connections between the categories that you have identified. What are the relationships between those categories? Are they of equal importance? Are there sociological theories that could help to interpret what is happening in the data? What does the literature say about the area you are researching and how do your own findings compare? Are you able to account for the similarities and for the differences?

While this may be the most creative phase, it is also, as Baptiste (2001) highlights, the most 'scary'. You can no longer hide behind the words of other people; you need to show how the findings from your study relate to findings from other studies, thus deepening our understanding of the area you are researching. You must be thinking that this sounds like a really big challenge: it is – but it is also extremely rewarding and can be fun.

Using software for qualitative data analysis

The method that has been described in previous sections describes a process that you can carry out without any particular data-analysis software. It involves very basic techniques: coloured pens, scissors, glue, pencils, a word-processing package and multiple copies of transcripts. This is a manual approach to data analysis. As with quantitative data analysis, there are software packages which can be used to help you manage the analysis. The tools these packages offer can help to organize, manage, search and code your data set. You need to remember, though, that they can only help your analysis – they will not do it for you. Deep engagement with the data will still involve you doing the thinking, and no computer package can do that for you.

One of the greatest benefits of qualitative data-analysis packages is their data-management functions. This means that they come into their own if you are working with large and complicated data sets. If you have never used qualitative-data-analysis software before and you are working with a small data set, you should ask yourself whether it is worth taking the time out of your dissertation to learn a package and what would be the advantages in doing so. If you've used qualitative-data-analysis packages before, if your institution has a licence for them, or if you hope to do more qualitative research in the future then there might be good reasons to give computer-aided analysis a try.

Unlike SPSS for quantitative data analysis, there is no market leader package for qualitative data analysis (Bryman 2004: 418). Most packages are able to support data management, coding and searching. Many are now able to deal with different types of data (for example, audio, visual and textual data). Lewins and Silver (2007) offer a comprehensive guide to qualitative data analysis using software, and it is worth a look if you choose to go down this route. Commonly used computer-aided qualitative-data-analysis packages include:

Nvivo;
ATLAS.ti;
HyperRESEARCH;
MAXQDA;
The Ethnograph;
Transana.

You will find an overview of these packages and links to their web pages on our website.

This list is not comprehensive. If you are considering using software to aid your data analysis, you should first see whether your institution holds a licence to one of the packages. If not, you'll need to do your homework to see which is the most appropriate for your work, timescale and budget.

Other approaches to qualitative data analysis

So far, we have described a very general approach to qualitative data analysis, which could loosely be described as thematic analysis. We have outlined a process of coding, categorization, theme development and comparison. This can be done manually or with the help of software packages.

There are, however, many other approaches to data analysis that you could use. Denzin and Lincoln's *The Sage Book of Qualitative Research* (2005) offers a comprehensive overview. Here we will focus on only some of them. A recommended text is given for each approach at the end of each subsection. This overview is not comprehensive but aims to give a feeling for some of the approaches that could be adopted.

Discourse analysis

Discourse analysis does not refer to one single approach; rather, it is a general term for approaches to the analysis of both written and spoken text. Different approaches to discourse analysis have grown out of different disciplines: linguistics, cognitive psychology and post-structuralism (Potter 2004: 201). Miller and Brewer (2003: 75–76) offer five broad categories of discourse analysis. The first is linguistic in focus and looks at discourse styles in social settings (such as school interactions, courtrooms, doctors' surgeries). The second looks at how language is used in natural situations – the 'ethnography of communication' and the competencies needed for that communication. The third category, conversation analysis, investigates how conversation is organized. The fourth focuses on the choice of words used in the textual and verbal accounts of social representatives. The fifth, critical discourse analysis, sees language as being bound up with power and ideology; analysis focuses on how language benefits certain groups over others.

These approaches all have different emphases, yet they all share the understanding that language is a social act that is embedded within a social context which both influences and is influenced by language (Gee 2005).

Grounded theory

Grounded theory (Glasser and Strauss 1967) aims to develop theory out of the data which has been collected. This is different to many approaches to research where a theoretical framework is chosen at the beginning of a project and then the data analysed in relation to that framework. The process of data collection, data analysis and theory generation in grounded theory are closely connected. The research question is set and sample selected. The data is collected and coded, and concepts are generated. The coding shows where more data needs to be collected. This process continues until there is saturation (that is, no more codes are emerging). Relationships between the categories are identified and a theory postulated. This substantive theory is then tested in different settings. This may lead to the development of a formal theory (Bryman 2004). The grounded-theory approach is not linear as it has been described here but is iterative and based on constant comparison, with different phases occurring simultaneously and being repeated.

Narrative analysis

Narrative analysis describes a suite of approaches that focuses on the analysis of the stories which people use to make sense of what Ezzy (2002) describes as disconnected episodes that together form a coherent construction of the past. The stories that narrative analysis analyses are the products of people who are living in a particular social, historical and cultural context; the stories they tell are a reflection of how they see themselves and others within their worlds (Lawler 2002). Narratives can be, among other things, used to give information, to structure our ideas about ourselves and to pass on experiences (Gibbs 2007: 60). Key examples of narratives are biographical and life-history accounts. There is little consensus on what narrative analysis involves, and Riessman has identified four different models (described in Bryman 2004: 412):

1   thematic (focus on what is said);
2   structural (focus on how it is said);
3   interactional (focus on the dialogue between teller and listener);
4   performative (focus on how the narrative is enacted).

Visual analysis

Visual analysis is used to analyse images which are both generated for the research study and also those which are already in existence.

Images can be 'researcher found' (generated by others) or 'researcher generated' (created by the researcher). Both are integral to the visual research process (Prosser 2006: 3).

These images can be used as either aides-memoires or as data in their own right (Bryman 2004: 312). Most analytical approaches that are used for non-image-based research can also be used for those which involve images (Banks 2007: 38). A researcher analysing images needs to be sensitive to the context in which they were generated, the potential for multiple meanings and the impact of their own role in production of the images (Bryman 2004; Banks 2007). There are approaches to analysis which may be particularly appropriate to the analysis of visual images, for example:

- semiotics – the study of signs and symbols to uncover their deeper meaning and how that meaning is understood (Chandler 1994);
- qualitative content analysis – finding underlying themes in the images being analysed and situating those findings within the context in which the images were produced;
- ethnomethodological approaches – identifying the everyday practices by which people organize their lives (Banks 2007: 49).

Case study: *Capturing a Telling Instance*

In this case study, Steve Spencer offers an analysis of an image of a scene in Darwin, Australia.

Figure 9.5 is a still from a short video (Spencer 2005). Analysis of the image reveals several complex themes. First, an analysis of the context: an 'alternative' market made up of food and craft stalls at a beach area in Darwin in northern Australia. It is a scene that shows tourists carrying takeaway food and drinking beer as they peruse a stall selling Aboriginal artefacts (a display of didgeridoos). The image by itself may seem mundane and not worthy of a second look. Yet, the themes of public drinking and commodification of Aboriginal culture could be explored further. The issue of public drinking is one which historically has been used as a derogatory stereotype of indigenous Australians (although statistically the problem of excessive drinking in the territory is much more likely to be white Australians, and only 30 per cent of Aboriginal people drink alcohol). However, there have been prohibitions imposed on indigenous public drinking. Interestingly, the pictured scene takes place 100 yards away from an annual event that celebrates white Australia's reverence for drinking – The Beer Can Regatta. Images like this are sometimes very significant because they demonstrate the everyday nature of long-standing social divisions and relationships of power.

Alongside this still image, the study added evidence about the representation of indigenous Australians, in news media (usually either as perpetrators or victims of crime), archive imagery showing demeaning stereotypes of indigenous people as drunks (see Spencer 2006: 149–151) and through interviews with people from an informal indigenous community near Darwin. Qualitative case studies increase in validity with the addition of several forms of evidence. As Banks (2007: 178) suggests: 'The study and use of visual images is only of use within broader sociological research enterprises, rather than as ends in themselves.'

Using imagery from events and social contexts like this captures the everyday nature of social divisions. While video is a powerful medium that conveys the immediacy and authenticity of experience, still images can capture a telling instance and allow time for critical reflection and analysis.

Figure 9.5 Picture from *Capturing a Telling Instance.*

(Steve Spencer)

These brief overviews of different approaches to data analysis have been designed to give you a taste of ways you can work with your data. If you choose to work with one of them, take a look at the recommended texts and also try and read a research paper which has adopted the same approach to analysis. This will show the ways in which the data analysis can be reported.

Checks on quality

In any research project, we want to be sure that our analysis is trustworthy. Miles and Huberman (1994: 277–280) offer five areas that should be explored to assess the quality of our work.

1 *Objectivity/confirmability.* Is the study relatively objective? Have the researcher's biases been acknowledged?
2 *Reliability/dependability/auditability.* Was the approach to the study consistent and stable over time?
3 *Internal validity/credibility/authenticity.* Do the findings make sense? Are they credible? Do they paint a true picture of what we were studying?
4 *External validity/transferability/fittingness.* How do these findings fit into the bigger picture? Can they be generalized to other settings?
5 *Utilization/application/action orientation.* What impact does the study have on the researchers and the researched?

For each of the areas above, Miles and Huberman offer a series of questions that could form the basis of reflection on your study and, therefore, a check on its quality.

Key messages

- There is no single approach and no 'right way' to do qualitative data analysis.
- Many approaches share four general phases: analysis definition, data classification, connection-making and message conveyance.
- Analysis involves interpretation – establishing links to theory, literature and experiences.
- Software packages can aid your analysis.
- Any approach to data analysis needs to undergo checks on quality.

Key questions

- Have you researched different approaches to data analysis? Do you understand what differentiates them?
- Are you able to justify why your chosen approach to data analysis is appropriate in terms of the data you have collected and also your view of research?
- Have you adopted a systematic approach to data classification? Have you been through the classification cycle more than once?
- In interpreting your data, have you moved beyond description? How do your findings fit with other work that is out there?
- Have you reflected honestly on your approach to data analysis? Where are the weaknesses and the strengths in what you have produced?

Further reading

Ball, M. and Smith, G. W. H. (1992) *Analyzing Visual Data*, London: Sage.

Bryman, A. (2004) *Social Research Methods*, 2nd edn, Oxford: Oxford University Press.

Charmaz, K. (2006) *Constructing Grounded Theory: A Practical Guide through Qualitative Data Analysis*, London: Sage.

Denzin, N. K. and Lincoln, Y. S. (2005) *The Sage Handbook of Qualitative Research*, London: Sage.

Gee, J. P. (2005) *An Introduction to Discourse Analysis: Theory and Method*, London: Routledge.

Lewins, A. and Silver, C. (2007) *Using Software in Qualitative Research: A Step-by-Step Guide*, London: Sage.

Pink, S. (2007) *Doing Visual Ethnography*, London: Sage.

Plummer, K. (2001) *Documents of Life 2: An Invitation to a Critical Humanism*, London: Sage.

Richards, L. (2005) *Handling Qualitative Data: A Practical Guide*, London: Sage.

Riessman, C. K. (1993) *Narrative Analysis*, Newbury Park, Calif.: Sage.

Silverman, D. (2006) *Interpreting Qualitative Data: Methods for Analysing Talk, Text and Interaction*, 3rd edn, London: Sage.

Chapter 10

Writing the dissertation

Introduction

By the time you start to write the first draft of your dissertation, you will probably already have accumulated a wealth of notes, scribblings and ideas about what you want to write about and possibly already collected some data. Your job is then to put all of those ideas into a coherent structure. This chapter sets out the component parts of a common format for a dissertation and how you can go about writing them. The importance of working with your supervisor's comments and proofreading are also highlighted. By the end of this chapter, you should have a better understanding of:

- how you can get started on the writing;
- the different parts of the dissertation and how you can approach them;
- how to prepare your dissertation for submission.

Producing a 'working title'

In so far as the preparation of the dissertation is a process of investigation and discovery, the precise scope of your study may well only emerge as you become closely involved in a detailed review of the literature. At this early stage, your title may be a provisional one, a 'working title', which you will revise later. Your dissertation supervisor may advise on the title in order to help you find and define the focus of the dissertation.

Planning the dissertation

It is highly advisable to draft a plan of the dissertation. There is a lot in common between different dissertations regarding the structure, and, although you do not need to stick slavishly to a standard plan, such a plan is very helpful as a template to impose some order on what may seem an unmanageable task.

> Splitting up the task into chapters, drawing up chapter plans and assigning a word count to each section really helped with this, so that when I started writing, I knew what I had to say, and how quickly I had to get to the point!

Another useful focusing device is to write a short abstract of about 300 words, in which you set out as clearly as possible what you intend to do in the dissertation. The value of this exercise is that it requires you to focus and articulate your thinking. You may be able to summarize the exact nature and scope of your study, in which case the abstract can serve as a guide to refer to as you write the main chapters of the work. Alternatively, it may make you aware of gaps in your knowledge and understanding and show you areas that need further thought and research. As you continue to write the main chapters of the work, you may find that your initial plan has changed. This means that when you have completed the chapters that form the main body of your dissertation, you may need to return to the abstract and revise it as much as you need to form the introduction.

It doesn't matter which chapter of your dissertation you write first. It is probably best to start with something that you feel confident about writing, whether that is the methods section, the literature review or the introduction. The rest of this chapter will outline some of the things that you could put in the different chapters.

Writing the introduction

The introduction may be the first chapter in your dissertation, but it doesn't have to be the first thing that you write. Having completed the work on the main substance of your dissertation, you should have a much clearer idea of its nature and scope than you did when you wrote your preliminary abstract or proposal. The introduction to your dissertation should explain to the reader what you are going to investigate. It should describe the dissertation's topic and scope. You should explain your reasons for investigating your chosen topic by referring to the appropriate literature.

It is important, however, to write the introduction as though you are setting out on a process of investigation. You need to emphasize the exploratory nature of your work. You should also avoid anticipating the discoveries and conclusions that you have made in the course of your investigations. So, you might simply say that you have identified certain common features in the relevant literature, or a particular issue that it deals with, and that your dissertation will examine the literature closely in order to demonstrate the relationships between treatments of the issue in the sample texts.

All texts are comprised of stages or 'moves' that a reader would recognize. Swales and Feak (2004: 244) have identified three distinct moves in the introductory sections of dissertations:

1   establishing a research territory;
2   establishing a niche;
3   occupying a niche.

Although Swales and Feak were writing for postgraduate students in the USA, much of what they say is relevant to undergraduate dissertations, and is extremely helpful in showing how the structures of the sections work. The three 'moves' are adapted in Figure 10.1. In Table 10.1, extracts

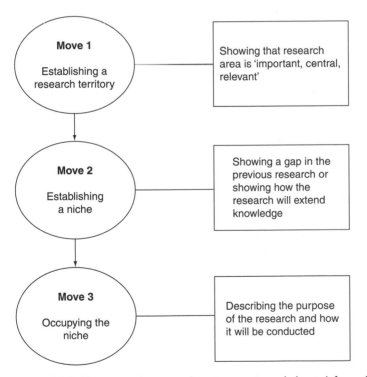

Figure 10.1 Moves in the introductory sections (adapted from Swales *et al.* 2004: 244).

Table 10.1 Examples of the introductory 'moves'

Move 1	'How people identify with others and their sense of belonging to social groups continues to be the subject of much academic and popular debate' (Southerton 2002: 171)
Move 2	'By contrast, Bourdieu's mechanisms for class-based identification are rigid and deny individuals the scope to change their consumption orientations and social group identification' (Southerton 2002: 172) 'More significantly, both sets of theories start from the premise that consumption is the most significant medium of identification' (Southerton 2002: 172)
Move 3	'To make headway in this debate it is important to step back from consumption and consider how the processes of identification operate' (Southerton 2002: 172) 'Boundaries are the point where group similarities end and differences begin. By analysing narratives of boundaries it is therefore possible to investigate identification without starting from the assumptions that consumption is the most significant medium' (Southerton 2002: 173) 'This article explores the boundaries advanced by research respondents in their narratives of identification and classification' (Southerton 2002: 173)

from the introductory section of Dale Southerton's article (2002) on social class, mobility and identification are used to highlight these moves.

These moves give you a really useful structure for writing your own dissertation introduction. It may help you to take a look at the introductory sections for six articles that you are reading for your literature review that relate to your dissertation topic. Use the list above as though it were a checklist and see how they are used. That will give you a sense of what is common practice in social sciences.

When you have completed the main body of the work and your tutor has commented on your complete draft, revisit the introduction to take into account your findings and your tutor's comments on their significance.

Writing a literature review

Hart (1998: 13) defines a literature review as:

> The selection of available documents (both published and unpublished) on the topic, which contain information, ideas, data and evidence written from a particular standpoint to fulfil certain aims or express certain views on the nature of the topic and how it is to be

investigated, and the effective evaluation of these documents in relation to the research being proposed.

It is your opportunity to offer a critical overview of the sources that you collected during the literature-searching phase of your dissertation. As we mentioned in Chapter 4, the literature review defines the context in which your research is situated and justifies why this is an important area to study. The literature review also allows you to demonstrate a number of skills that you have acquired: literature searching, a broad understanding of your topic and the methods you have chosen for its research (Hart 1998: 13).

It is important to remember that a literature review is different to an annotated bibliography. An annotated bibliography lists the sources that you have identified and offers a summary of them one by one. A literature review, in contrast, will make comparisons between references, identify links and note developments in your subject area.

There are different ways in which you can group the literature in your review. Three of the most common approaches include chronological, thematic and methodological.

- In a *chronologically* organized review, you order your review around the development through time of your area of interest. Cottrell (2003: 204) suggests looking for 'chains' – that is how the pieces of research link to and develop others. These developments can then be charted.
- In a *thematically* organized review, the literature is presented around emergent issues or topics. Such a presentation of literature will highlight what the main themes are in your area of study. When conducting this kind of review, you will have to extract the key points from each source and look for connections with the other literature you have reviewed. The review will be presented through a series of sections and subsections.
- In *methodologically* organized reviews, the focus is on the methods used by the researcher to carry out his or her research rather than on the content of the research. Such a review will be appropriate if you are looking to develop knowledge about a method or an approach to research.

Whichever approach you adopt, you should see that the literature review ends by showing where your own research will add to the knowledge base in your area of interest. Organizing your review chronologically, thematically or methodologically will also bring your empirical or theoretical work into sharper focus. You are prefacing your work and how it relates to other academic studies by your discussion of it in your literature review. In the discussion section of your study, you will relate your findings to those central studies that you have highlighted in your literature review.

Often students ask how long a literature review should be. This is a difficult question given that the total length of your dissertation might be anything from 5,000 to 8,000 words. Ask your supervisor to give some indication of an appropriate length for your literature review. Although you will worry about reaching the required number of words, don't become preoccupied with word length. It is not unusual that you will first get down lots of words and then have to cut them back – many people work this way; however, you must capture and critically evaluate the key literature in your topic area. In summary, your literature review should:

- demonstrate that you understand your topic area;
- include all seminal texts;
- lead into your proposed research;
- make conclusions about what has already been written;
- introduce the definitions and approaches that shape your topic area;
- offer recommendations based on your reading;
- identify any gaps in knowledge (Hart 1998: 198).

Writing the methods section

The methods section is often the easiest chapter of your dissertation to write. In the methods section, you are telling the reader what you did in your study. Since it is often straightforward to write, you might decide to do this chapter first. Since you are discussing something that has already happened, you should write this section in the *past tense*: for example, 'I interviewed eight people' or 'eight people were interviewed' rather than 'I will interview eight people' or 'eight people will be interviewed'.

The methods section must clearly identify the epistemological and ontological basis of the study and demonstrate a good working knowledge of the methods to be employed. It should include good coverage of the process of the fieldwork and indicate how the analysis was undertaken. As well as covering the ethical issues, it should also contain an element of reflection on the research process. At all stages, you should be making reference to research methods literature.

Here is a list of questions that you should ask yourself as you are writing the methods section:

- Have you stated your hypothesis or research questions clearly?
- Have you clearly outlined how you designed your research?
- Have you evaluated the type of data that you have collected?
- Have you evaluated and justified the method you have chosen?
- Have you explained the procedure you followed?
- Have you mentioned the equipment you used and the conditions under which you carried out your research?
- Have you described how you will analyse the data?

Writing the findings and results section

Many students confuse findings with discussion, and it is important to keep them separate, at least in your mind. In the findings section, you are presenting what you have found in your research and what you interpret those findings to mean. The discussion section is where you link your data analysis back to literature you introduced in your literature review. Some dissertation guidance will put the two together in one chapter, others will ask for separate chapters. Check what is required at your university.

In your findings section, it is important that you present your results in a logical and convincing manner. If your results are presented in a confusing way, the reader will not follow your argument and may not trust your conclusions.

If you are presenting quantitative data, there are a number of things that you should consider. First, have you used the most appropriate way of presenting your data? Nominal data, for example, is best represented numerically by a frequency table and graphically by a pie chart; ordinal data often looks better with a bar chart representation; and for interval or ratio data, a frequency table will probably be very large, so a histogram would be better here. Whenever you introduce a table or chart into your dissertation, you need to ensure that this is clearly labelled with a title and a figure or table number. Make sure that all of the data that you present is interpreted. It is not sufficient to just describe it. One common mistake that people make is that they merely repeat what is in the graphs in words. This is not interpretation, it is description. You also need to ensure that you refer to all of the tables and charts somewhere in the text. If not, you need to ask yourself why those tables and charts are there.

When it comes to qualitative data, there are no fixed rules about the best way to present qualitative data. Miles and Huberman (1994: 304) offer the following advice: 'A good report should provide basic data, preferably in a focused form (vignettes, organized narrative, photographs, or our data displays) so that the reader, can, in parallel with the researcher, draw warranted conclusions.'

This means that you need to choose extracts from your data that evidence the arguments you are making in your data analysis. These can be, for example, quotes from your interviews or focus groups or notes or photographs from your observations. Quotes and other raw data will bring your analysis to life and will make your findings more credible. As with quantitative data analysis, you should clearly label your data extracts. For interview data, you may choose to give your interviewees pseudonyms (made-up names) or you might decide to number the interviews. You should set your quotes apart from the rest of the text by indenting them. Below is an example (taken from Todd *et al.* 2006: 169) of how an extract from an interview study could be included in the text. The extract is from an interview with an undergraduate dissertation tutor talking about her experiences of supervision. The interviewee is given a number (2), but she could easily have been given a pseudonym (Dr Pilcher).

> I think that my role isn't to get involved in the writing of content but you're looking for ways to facilitate what they're doing and that might mean, for some of the weaker students, some direct intervention. (2)

Whether your results are quantitative, qualitative or a mixture of both, there are some things to bear in mind:

- Have you given a clear overview of what you have found out from your research?
- Have you included any data which are not needed?
- Have you interpreted your data and not just described it?
- Have you labelled all your tables, figures and quotes?

Writing the discussion section

Traditionally, the discussion links findings to the literature presented in the literature review. The discussion section is the place where you show the significance of your findings and highlight what has been achieved when compared to the original aims. There are arguments for extending the coverage of literature in this section but only in exceptional circumstances, such as when you have obtained completely different results to what you expected. The discussion should be an opportunity to raise the different voices of interest in the research question and to explore the findings in the light of the literature and different perspectives within it.

In a piece of small-scale research, Swales and Feak (2004: 270–272) identified the following different ways to open the discussion section:

- citing the main results;
- discussing the literature;
- offering general conclusions;
- reminding the reader about the original purpose;
- highlighting the special importance of the research site;
- focusing on the methodology;
- discussing the limitations of the research.

Look at some discussion section openings in articles that relate to your topic area. Doing this will give you a sense of what happens in your field. When you write your own discussion section, you can use the same opening strategy.

Writing the conclusion

The main chapters of your dissertation will have focused on particular topics or issues. For example, each chapter may have focused discussion on a particular text. Alternatively, you may have structured your work so that each chapter is devoted to discussion of a particular aspect of your overall topic. The conclusion offers the opportunity to review your work as a whole, to identify the points of comparison and contrast the various texts you have examined, and to show that, in the process of your study, you have developed a more precise, critical understanding of the way they deal with your topic. This is also an appropriate place for you to point to the potential limitations of small-scale research of this kind and to indicate possible avenues for researchers to address the issues in the future. Don't worry about being critical of your work; it shows that you can take a step back and look at your work with a reflective eye – markers love this. We often don't spend enough time writing the conclusion because it comes right at the end when we are tired. But this is your chance to finish your dissertation on a really strong note, so you should plan time to do it well.

Here is a simple exercise which might help you:

- read through your dissertation slowly;
- highlight the main points with a highlighter;
- summarize these points on sticky labels;
- sequence the labels and use them to write your conclusion.

Revising sections after receiving the supervisor's comments

When you have received your supervisor's comments on the draft of any chapter, you should revise that particular chapter immediately. Prompt revision is easier than letting things drift, and you should do it while the advice of your supervisor is fresh in your mind. This will also avoid building up a backlog of work that needs to be revised, which can be discouraging. Having the material on a computer will enable you to do revisions efficiently and with a minimum of fuss. But take care of your work: be sure to back up what you have done on a floppy disk, CD or memory stick. This is really important. We have known students who have lost everything they have done due to a computer meltdown, which almost caused them to melt down themselves!

Final draft

The process of preparing your dissertation for submission begins with a careful final reading of all your chapters and sections. Here you have the opportunity:

- to ensure that your argument is clearly developed from sentence to sentence, from paragraph to paragraph and from chapter to chapter;
- to check the accuracy of your spelling and punctuation (do not rely on spellchecker software!);
- to make sure that your sentences are well constructed and that you are expressing yourself clearly, precisely and fluently;
- to ensure that you have not contradicted or repeated yourself;
- to check whether your working title adequately describes the content of your dissertation and whether you need to change it.

You need to check that your quotations from and references to both primary and secondary texts are clearly and consistently identified according to the conventions of the referencing systems your department requires. There is more about this in Chapter 11. You should check your references both ways: see that all the references in your dissertation are in your reference list and that all the references in your reference list are in the dissertation.

Guidelines on presentation

You should refer to the guidance provided by your own department, but, in general, you should think about the following:

- the dissertation must have a table of contents;
- the pages of the dissertation must be numbered;
- it must have a title page, including the title, your name, the award and the date;
- there should be consistency in terms of style and layout.

Proofreading

Your final task before you submit should be to proofread your dissertation. In this final stage, you will be looking for grammatical and typographical errors. At this point, you will have read your dissertation a number of times, so it will be very familiar to you. You, therefore, need to use strategies to help you see your dissertation through different eyes. If you have been drafting thus far on your computer, print out a copy of the dissertation as mistakes are often easier to spot when in print. Read your dissertation out loud and see whether what you are saying makes sense. You could also read through concentrating on the grammar and spelling rather than the content. Doing this makes you look at each word individually, rather than skim-reading which is what people tend to do. When you have read through the whole dissertation, make any necessary changes and then go back to check the layout and presentation guidelines given by your institution to ensure that your dissertation is in the correct format. Then you can print the final copy and have it bound (if required).

One of my supervisors mentioned that her Masters students wrote better and more coherently when they thought their target audience weren't social scientists, so I asked people who were not involved with my course to proofread my drafts. If they understood what I was getting at, I figured I wasn't going too far wrong! And then, obviously, dissertation supervisors or friends from your course can comment on the academic style of your writing too, so you'll have it covered from both sides!

Submitting the completed dissertation

The completed dissertation should be submitted in the form set out by your department. If there are no formal styles, submit the dissertation in a format that makes it easy for the examiner to handle – avoid complicated spring-back or ring-backed files. And when you have submitted, it is time to go out and celebrate!

Key messages

- Depending on the rules and regulations of your own institution, give your supervisor drafts of chapters as you write them, and try to be responsive to criticism. Revise chapters as soon as you get them back.
- Even if you write the introduction last, write it as if you have yet to find the answers to your questions.
- Finally, check that the title refers accurately to the finished dissertation. If it does not, change the title.
- Check how your department wants you to present your work.

Key questions

- Have you mapped out the content of each of your chapters?
- In what order will the content flow best?
- Is your discussion doing its job? Likewise, is your conclusion suitably conclusive?
- Is the order of the chapters logical and coherent, will it make sense to the reader? Are any sections of the dissertation repetitive or contradictory?
- Do you know someone else who can proofread the dissertation for you?

Further reading

Beard, C. (2005) *Mastering University*, Abingdon: Gower.

Bryman, A. (2008) *Social Research Methods*, 3rd edn, Oxford: Oxford University Press.

Cottrell, S. (2003) *Skills for Success*, Basingstoke: Palgrave-Macmillan.

Denscombe, M. (2002) *The Good Research Guide for Small-Scale Social Research Projects*, Buckingham: Open University Press.

Swales, J. M. and Feak, C. B. (2004) *Academic Writing for Graduate Students*, Ann Arbor, Mich.: University of Michigan Press.

Chapter 11

Finding your academic voice in your writing

Introduction

You will be assessed not only on the intellectual content of your dissertation but also on the way you put across your academic argument. This means that your written style is incredibly important. The success with which you convey your ideas will depend significantly upon the fluidity of your writing style. Writing a dissertation involves following a formula; to be successful, the dissertation must adhere to those accepted rules of academic writing. A wide range of resources and guidance are available to help improve academic style; here we will give you guidance on how to finesse your academic writing.

By the end of this chapter, you should have a better understanding of:

- academic discourse and your entrance into the academic community;
- the writing process;
- finding the right style;
- plagiarism;
- citing and referencing.

What is academic discourse?

During your time as an undergraduate, you may have become aware of a style of presentation that has slowly influenced your essay writing. However, this may never have been taught to you explicitly. Reading academic textbooks and journal articles, attending lectures and being part of a student community have exposed you to a habit of writing that might be termed 'academic discourse'.

You will have already begun to assimilate some principles of this style into your own work. Do not be alarmed at the notion of assimilation. This is not a covert ploy to enforce the rules of a language police upon your creativity, nor is it about restricting your expression, interest and understanding of a subject. Academic discourse is simply a set of norms and conventions, habits of writing, which make your work intelligible, interesting and engaging to your reader. It assumes that writers and readers form part of a community and can discuss concepts and theories that can be explained, examined and, if necessary, contested, within mutually understood boundaries of communication. This last sentence verges on abstraction but, simply put, means that an academic discourse contains its own conventions about how to present research and how to read and respond to research. The problem is that the requirements of academic discourse are often implicit. As a student you are expected to gain a grasp of academic literacy without necessarily being given directed instruction in how to employ these conventions in your own academic writing.

So, although this chapter talks about finding your own academic voice, we recognize that expression in your own voice when writing academically is difficult because of the norms and conventions mentioned above. Instead, you should be 'making choices from a range of alternatives within academic writing trying to find ones which are most in harmony with [your] sense of [yourself]' (Ivanic and Simpson 1992: 142). It's a bit like great classical composers. Composers work within the same parameters of instrumentation, dynamics and harmony. What different composers produce is recognizable as music. But the music of Mozart is different to that of Holst, which is different again to the music of Vivaldi. As you write more, you will become aware of your own style, a style which is executed within the boundaries of the social sciences.

The process of academic writing

All writing is tailored to an audience which shares certain conventions of style and grammar. Newspapers represent an obvious example of how one area of writing practice (journalism) can have so many variations in discourse. Without delving into issues of power, representation or political bias, it is worth noting that academic essays require a certain formality that places the writer in the background and allows the exposition of a carefully worked argument to come to the fore.

As a student of the social sciences, your dissertation may include statistics, graphs or other representations of data, and it may include multimedia components as well as text. However, in addition to presenting data, your aim is to persuade the reader that you have understood the processes of research and can present that research in a clear and intelligible manner.

Sitting down to write your dissertation might seem like an impossible task. It is likely that you have never had to write anything this long before. It is, therefore, useful to see your dissertation writing as a process that can be carried out in smaller, more manageable chunks rather than trying to write it all at once. It is easier to write when you have planned, researched and organized your thinking already. However, don't wait until you have built up absolutely everything before you write, as your writing of drafts also serves the purpose of developing your thoughts as you go along. Indeed, you are likely to produce a number of drafts of your dissertation before you submit it. For example:

- The first draft sketches an overview of the dissertation and breaks up the presentation of findings into appropriate chapters. This draft should be written quickly and should not focus too much on the standard of your English. The aim is to get some words on the paper.
- The second draft revises your arguments, enhances the exposition of your thesis and begins the check for grammatical ambiguities.
- The third draft corrects punctuation and errors in referencing in accordance with your particular course requirements and, if necessary, rearranges some of the content.
- The fourth draft clarifies any remaining arguments.

You may write even more than four drafts. Becker (cited in Cooper *et al.* 1998: 253) had a hard job convincing his students that he would usually work on eight to ten drafts of a manuscript for publication: 'Do not try and get it right the first time – even if it sounds cumbersome or not quite right, it's better to get something down that you can then re-read and bash into shape.'

The above is an indication of the possible stages of writing and merely illustrates the process of reworking your essay, a task which is often avoided, because of the time factor involved, but which is essential if you are to produce a quality dissertation that does justice to your research. We recommend that the main revisions should take place between the first and second draft. It is useful here to get someone else to look at your work in progress. This might be your dissertation supervisor, but it could also be a friend from your course. You should pay attention to their comments and see whether you can make the changes that they suggest.

It is also worth leaving a time gap between each draft. This gives you the opportunity to take a break from your work and to come back to it with fresh eyes. Don't worry, you will still be working on your dissertation, because you will continue to process the ideas and arguments of your thesis in your head, but you will not be constrained by the printed word in front of you. Making time for these breathing spaces when writing your dissertation requires good time planning and time management throughout the dissertation process – it won't work if you sit down to write at the last minute. If you can, it is always a good idea to try to finish some time before any final deadlines.

In the next section we'll look at how you can develop your academic writing.

Adopting a suitable writing style

Acquiring the ability to write academic essays is a developmental process which improves during the course of your studies. This chapter is not intended to be a comprehensive overview of grammatical usage and style. So, if you have problems with your grammar, punctuation and spelling (for example you struggle with the difference between 'it's' and 'its' or 'their', 'there' and 'they're' or if you don't know when it's best to use a semi-colon rather than a comma), take a look at some of the more broad texts on English grammar, which are recommended at the end of this section.

Here we'll look at issues of style, focusing on:

- formality;
- clarity, conciseness and precision;
- objectivity.

Formality

Academic writing is formal. It does not have to be stuffy and complicated, but it does need to be written formally. Here are some pointers:

- Avoid using slang, for example: 'the intervention went down a treat', 'the fieldwork was dicey'.
- Don't use contractions. Instead of 'don't', use 'do not'; instead of 'can't' use 'cannot'; instead of 'should've' use 'should have', etc. You'll have noticed that we have used contractions in this book. This is because the norms and conventions are different for study guides and dissertations. Study guides tend to be less formal than academic essays.
- The same is true for abbreviations. These should also be written out in full:
  - e.g. = for example
  - no. = number
  - i.e. = that is

- You can, however, use recognized acronyms, as long as you define them on their first occurrence:
  - Gross Domestic Product (GDP);
  - Statistics Package for the Social Sciences (SPSS);
  - British National Party (BNP).
- Numbers below 100 should be written in full: eleven interviewees; forty-nine students. If you use percentages or other units of measurement, however, you can leave them in figures: 99 per cent.

Clarity, conciseness and precision

It is usually easier to identify clear, concise writing by looking at examples of sentences which are confusing and misleading. One key area of difficulty for students, when writing 'academic discourse', is the use of active and passive constructions. Essentially, these constructions affect the ordering of the relationship between the subject, object and verb elements of a sentence. Passive constructions can often be spotted by noticing the use of the verb 'to be' with the past participle of a transitive verb. For example, 'The cause of the social groupings was [past tense of the verb 'to be'] determined.'

The problem with passive sentences is that the subject of the sentence can disappear, making the sentence vague. It is not clear in this example who determined the cause of the social groupings. Was it the writer of the dissertation? Or perhaps other scholars? If it was determined by the work of other scholars, then those scholars need to be referenced.

The above sentence could be written using the active voice. Written this way, you will have to decide whether you are giving your own judgement or that of another person because the sentence needs to have a subject: 'We determined the cause of the social groupings.'

Here, it was the authors who determined the cause of the groupings, but it could easily have been another writer, for example, Karl Marx, depending on the argument being put forward.

The above example may be extreme, but it highlights some basic grammatical principles which, if followed, help to present academic research clearly. For many students, writing under other pressures, spending time converting all passive constructions into active phrases will be excruciating and needless. In fact, there is often a tendency to use passive constructions when the writer is not quite sure of how to express a particular idea or concept or has only partially conceptualized the principle of research to be discussed (passive constructions can also be used inappropriately as filler to make up word count).

There is an important caveat here. Passive constructions are abundant in academic writing, and an essay full of active sentences will not translate into a recognizable academic essay. As in most things, a considered balance to your writing, and a reflective approach, will aid in communicating your results most effectively.

Other aspects that will make your writing more precise and concise include:

- Leave out needless words. Try to avoid phrases such as 'It can be seen at this point of the enquiry that...' Again, you will find examples of these phrases in journals and textbooks; however, for the sake of clarity in your own work, it is better to keep a limit on them.
- Use specific terms rather than abstractions. Show your mastery of technical concepts relevant to your discipline, but try not to over-complicate the explanations of these terms in relation to your research. Remember that your immediate audience will be your peers and tutoring staff, who will know the theories and terminologies specific to your area of study.
- Choose words with precision. This sounds obvious, but if you are not clear about the choice of words then your dissertation reader may get the impression that you have not thought enough about the topic under discussion. Use a dictionary to make sure that you are using a word correctly.
- Use alternatives to common words. This is a basic principle for all forms of writing and helps to avoid monotony. The most frequent use of this will be when using pronouns (I, he, she, we, it, they, that) to replace the subject of a sentence. Related to this is the concept of 'elegant variation', which some view as rhetoric or studied avoidance for the sake of clear exposition. The best approach is to balance your writing with synonyms – use the synonym feature in Microsoft Word to help you with this.

Objectivity

Academic discourse avoids the use of words which are subjective and personal. These are statements such as 'very interesting', 'extremely useful', 'excellent'. Such constructions are not used because you cannot be certain whether you and your reader will interpret these words in the same way. Although questions of objectivity or subjectivity are crucial to social science research, the evidence from your research forms the basis of any evaluation rather than through qualifying statements.

One of the questions that many students ask is whether they can use 'I' in their dissertations. One of the reasons for not using 'I' is that it can be seen as too subjective or idiosyncratic, for example: 'I think Nelson Mandela symbolizes freedom and equality.' The problem with this statement is that there is no justification for giving Mandela this accolade. If, however, the writer had or was about to provide evidence to support this statement, there would be no problem with the use of 'I'. The problem, then, is not with 'I' but with the argument that supports that 'I'. Academic writing requires you to make personal judgements about the things you are discussing; yet, as with other aspects of academic writing, it is sensible not to overuse 'I', restricting it to the following situations:

1   when you need to make it clear to the reader that a judgement is your own and not to be confused with that of an author whose judgement you have been reporting or discussing, or when you want to emphasize where you stand with respect to other work;
2   when you wish to emphasize your own degree of confidence in the outcome of your reasoning;
3   when you want to announce to the reader how you propose to proceed or what modes of analysis you are engaging in.

(Taylor 1989: 144–145)

Because there is so much debate about whether 'I' should be used, it is worth discussing this with your supervisor. They might have very strong beliefs about this issue, which will be worth you knowing before you start to write.

This section has shown the importance of using evidence in your writing to substantiate any claims that you make. In the next section, we look at how the evidence of others should be treated in your dissertation.

Respecting the voices of others

In Western academic culture, there is the underlying belief that academic endeavour aims to build knowledge and that knowledge builds on knowledge already generated by others (through using that knowledge, borrowing it, modifying it or disregarding it). When producing new knowledge, it is understood that the originators of previous knowledge need to be recognized and acknowledged. If you do not do this and you use other people's ideas, words, thoughts or work without acknowledgement, then you are plagiarizing. It is unlikely that you will have reached the final year of your degree programme without hearing the word 'plagiarism', but it is worth recapping what plagiarism is and how you can ensure that your work is produced honestly, fairly and with respect of those who came before you, in keeping with the values that the Western academic community holds dear.

What is plagiarism?

The formal regulations governing cheating and plagiarism will be detailed in your departmental or institutional literature. You should consult these regulations to find out the specific definition of cheating and plagiarism for your institution. Cheating can include things such as falsifying data and making false declarations about yourself in order to get special treatment (for example, pretending to be ill to get an extension). Plagiarism is when you try and pass someone else's words or ideas off as your own. It is often defined as being either intentional or unintentional. Intentional plagiarism means knowingly using someone else's work (for example, buying work from another person or an essay bank, or colluding with another student) without acknowledging this. Sometimes a lack of understanding about how to reference can lead you to plagiarize accidentally. This is unintentional plagiarism and results in using sentences from someone else's work without acknowledgement. Unintentional plagiarism was a real concern for the student that took part in a research project about plagiarism:

> When I first started I was again unsure what to do in terms of references and that sort of thing. So you could say that in some of my essays I did things wrong unknowingly because I didn't reference it right. But that was something to do with my lack of experience in academia.
>
> (Ashworth *et al.* 1997: 192)

There are many reasons why students plagiarize (intentionally or unintentionally). These include:

* not leaving enough time to do the work themselves;
* poor study skills (for example, note-taking, summarizing, referencing);
* lack of confidence in ability to write in English;
* confusion about what plagiarism is.

There are, however, grave penalties for being caught plagiarizing, which could ultimately result in you not gaining your degree at the end of the course. Tutors are becoming more adept at spotting plagiarism (often aided by plagiarism detection services such as the Turnitin programme), so, you should do your utmost to ensure that your writing is your own, and what is not your own is acknowledged.

We cannot condone intentional cheating and plagiarism for any reason. But we can offer guidance on how to avoid unintentional plagiarism. In the next section we'll introduce how to cite and reference correctly.

Working with other people's words

It is not always clear how to work with other people's words, as this dissertation student shows: 'I think sometimes I'm confused the aim is I erm get the words get the ideas from other people and then I can't use their words (laughs) so have I copied?' (Pilcher 2007: 211).

We aim to make attribution clearer here. There are different ways in which you can incorporate words and ideas of another person into your dissertation: summary, paraphrase and direct quotation. In this section, we'll use an extract from Sue Wilkinson's chapter on focus group research in David Silverman's (2004) edited collection on *Qualitative Research*. Here is the full extract.

> Focus groups have a number of distinct advantages over one-to-one interviews. Most obviously, they provide a way of collecting data relatively quickly from a large number of participants. More importantly, focus groups are more 'naturalistic' than interviews (i.e. closer to everyday conversation) in that they typically include a range of communication purposes – such as storytelling, joking, arguing, boasting, teasing, persuasion, challenge and disagreement. The dynamic quality of group interaction, as participants discuss, debate, and (sometimes) disagree, is generally a key feature of focus groups.
>
> (Wilkinson 2004: 180)

In a summary, you list the main points of the work, in your own words, including a reference. Here is the extract summarized:

Following Wilkinson (2004), the main advantages that focus groups have compared to one-to-one interviews are:

- *They enable you to get more data from more people more quickly.*
- *They are closer to normal conversations.*
- *They allow for interaction between the participants.*

Like a summary, when you paraphrase, you outline, in your own words, what the author said. While a summary will pick out the key points of what has been said, in a paraphrase you are putting the original into a new form. The benefit of paraphrasing is that it pushes you to show that you have really understood what you have read. As with summarizing, you need to acknowledge the original source. Here is the extract paraphrased:

> *When compared to individual interviews, focus groups have some specific advantages. They allow the researcher to collect data from more participants in less time. Another important feature of focus group discussions is that they are more like natural conversations than the discussions in interviews, with participants telling jokes, persuading, and challenging each other, for example. A further characteristic of focus groups is the dynamism of the interactions between participants, who actively discuss, examine, and even argue.*
>
> *(Wilkinson 2004)*

You can use the exact words from the original text. When you use a direct quotation in your coursework, make sure that you put it in inverted commas and, if it is a lengthy quotation (more than three lines), indent it so that it appears separate from your own words. You should also include the page number from the original source. Here are two examples of how direct quotes from the extract could be used.

Example 1

> *Wilkinson (2004: 180) highlights an important feature of focus groups as being that they are 'more "naturalistic" than interviews (i.e. closer to everyday conversation) in that they typically include a range of communication purposes'.*

Example 2

> *Wilkinson (2004: 180) outlines the conversational element of focus groups:*
>
> > *Focus groups are more 'naturalistic' than interviews (i.e. closer to everyday conversation) in that they typically include a range of communication purposes – such as storytelling, joking, arguing, boasting, teasing, persuasion, challenge and disagreement. The dynamic quality of group interaction, as participants discuss, debate, and (sometimes) disagree, is generally a key feature of focus groups.*

Try to avoid very lengthy quotes. If you find that you want to use long quotes, consider using a summarizing or paraphrasing technique instead.

The final example is of a plagiarized version of the extract.

Example 3

Focus groups have some distinct advantages over one-to-one interviews. They provide a way of collecting data relatively quickly from a large number of participants. They are more 'naturalistic' than interviews (i.e. closer to everyday conversation).

Here, the original author, Wilkinson, is not acknowledged. Some words have been changed ('some' rather than 'a number of'), but the extract is neither summarized nor paraphrased. There are a number of direct quotations that are not in quotation marks. In presenting work such as the above, you are not respecting Sue Wilkinson's scholarship, and you are acting academically dishonestly in passing off the words and ideas as your own.

Referencing

You should aim to improve your study skills. As we highlighted in Chapter 4, when you are reading, get into the habit of noting down the exact source of what you have read. You need to include details of the following:

- author;
- year of publication;
- article or journal title;
- book title;
- place of publication;
- publisher;
- page numbers.

Keeping these detailed notes will save you a lot of time when it comes to preparing your reference list. In the reference list, there is an accepted format for presenting those references. There are many different ways to present your references, you should check at your institution which format they expect. Many institutions will use a version of Harvard (as does this book). A straightforward book reference in Harvard looks like this:

Bryman, A. (2004) *Social Research Methods*, Oxford: Oxford University Press.

There will be slight differences between this and how you present chapters from books, journal articles and online resources. You need to follow the guidelines given to you by your university. Correct referencing is not difficult, but some find it tedious to do. You need to be systematic, consistent and pay close attention to detail (making sure, for example, that all the references have full stops in the correct places).

Given that producing a reference list is not an intellectual endeavour, you might consider using bibliographic packages such as Endnote or Refworks to help you. In these packages, you input the bibliographical data into a database. It is then possible to choose the referencing style that you require, and the package will automatically convert your reference list into the correct format, ensuring consistency. This might save you a lot of time.

Correct referencing or citing other sources is not just about avoiding allegations of plagiarism:

- Referencing gives authority to your work, supporting the point you are making or adding weight to your argument.
- It demonstrates your understanding of a particular issue; recognizing the significance of other people's views increases that of your own.
- Properly referencing material in assignments can improve the overall quality of presentation as well as enhance the content. But don't overdo it – consult your supervisor for guidance.

Key messages

- Observe basic grammatical conventions.
- Read articles written in your discipline so you get a feel for the way in which your subject is written about.
- Remember the audience you are writing for. Academic work requires a certain formality and the need to develop a carefully worked argument.
- Write with integrity, showing respect for your own work and the work of others and always credit your sources and keep a full bibliography and references.
- Leave time to draft, redraft and proofread your work.

Key questions

- Based on feedback from previous assessments, what are your strengths in writing?
- Are you clear about the rules of academic style you need to follow?
- If you are unsure about your style, have you sought advice from your

supervisor or other support within your university (student services, the library, etc.)?

- Have you referenced all of your quotations?
- Is it clear when you are citing the work of others and when you are presenting your own views/conclusions?

Further reading

Grammar

Crystal, D. (2004) *Rediscover Grammar*, Harlow: Longman.

Seely, J. (2007) *Oxford A–Z of Grammar and Punctuation*, Oxford: Oxford University Press.

Writing

Pears, R. and Shield, G. (2005) *Cite Them Right: The Essential Guide to Referencing and Plagiarism*, 5th edn, Newcastle-Upon-Tyne: Pear Tree Books.

Redman, P. (2006) *Good Essay Writing: A Social Sciences Guide*, London: Sage.

Chapter 12

Beyond submission
Making the most of your dissertation

Introduction

When you hand in your dissertation, you may feel as if it is the last time you want to look at it. All the hard work is over, and now you can celebrate! While assessment is the driving reason for doing the dissertation, as a substantive piece of work, the more benefits you can reap from it the better.

This final chapter offers you some ideas about ways in which you can maximize the work you have undertaken for your dissertation. By the end of this chapter, you will have a better understanding of:

- how to reflect on and evidence your graduate attributes;
- drawing on your dissertation in job applications;
- using your dissertation in applications for more advanced levels of study;
- disseminating your dissertation more widely;
- resubmitting should you not reach a pass standard.

Graduate attributes and employability

The growth of mass higher education globally has resulted in changes to patterns of employment among graduates (Stewart and Knowles 1999; Holmes *et al.* 1998) and more competition for jobs. While at university, you will have developed a range of skills and attributes through the learning, teaching and assessment activities that you have experienced and also through your participation in extra-curricular activities (for example, volunteering, work experience and sports' club membership).

This focus on graduate attributes and employability has resulted in a number of useful frameworks for reflecting on what you have achieved and learned from your degree, including your dissertation. Identifying and articulating your strengths and competences will be helpful to you in seeking work or higher study.

Denholm *et al.* (2003: 6–7) define four facets to employability that can help you think about what you have learned and how you can make the best use of that learning.

1   Assets (the knowledge, skills and attitudes embodied by the employable graduate).
2   Deployment (the strategies and dispositions of the employable graduate).
3   Presentation (the ability of the graduate to demonstrate their assets and dispositions to employers).
4   Context (the personal and wider social and economic context in which the graduate is seeking work).

Figure 12.1 is a model for an effective self-review approach, showing the interface between personal, career and academic facets to learning.

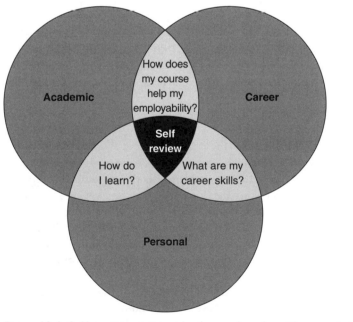

Figure 12.1 Self-review approach (reproduced with permission of QAA).

QAA Scotland (2006) defines graduate attributes that may be developed or enhanced through research activities such as the dissertation:

- critical understanding informed by current developments in the subject;
- an awareness of the provisional nature of knowledge, how knowledge is created, advanced and renewed and the excitement of changing knowledge;
- the ability to identify and analyse problems and issues and to formulate, evaluate and apply evidence-based solutions and arguments;
- an ability to apply a systematic and critical assessment of complex problems and issues;
- an ability to deploy techniques of analysis and enquiry;
- familiarity with advanced techniques and skills;
- originality and creativity in formulating, evaluating and applying evidence-based solutions and arguments;
- an understanding of the need for a high level of ethical, social, cultural, environmental and wider professional conduct.

These may be helpful for you to consider when trying to reflect upon and summarize what you have learned as part of your dissertation.

If you are a student in the UK, you may find that you are encouraged to link your personal development plans (PDP) to your dissertation. 'The process is intended to help individuals understand the value added through learning that is above and beyond attainment in the subjects they have studied' (QAA online).

Job applications

Dissertations usually represent the final piece of assessed work within an academic programme and, as such, are symbolic of both progression and ending. The next step after completing the dissertation may be applying for jobs. So, how can you use the experience of dissertation writing when applying for jobs?

Competence-based interview techniques are popular, and the type of information requested at the application stage will be competence-based too, so you want to try and ensure that your application form details and examples are reflected at the interview stage.

Your dissertation is about developing skills in research and analysis. When you write your CV, you have to show both the evidence of skills developed and a source of examples so you can demonstrate exactly *how* you have developed these skills and used them in previous work.

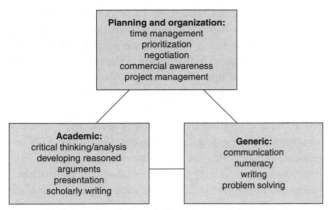

Figure 12.2 Employability skills enhanced through dissertation work.

In a competence-based interview, you may be asked about *situations* that demonstrate *skills* you have utilized. So, as a major piece of independent study, you may wish to use your dissertation to highlight skills in a range of areas as shown in Figure 12.2.

Typical questions you may be asked to discuss are:

- a situation when something happened;
- an example of when you did something (for example, dealt with a complex problem);
- what would you do to deal with specific situations.

When you answer these types of question, think about:

- the situation or context;
- the task;
- the action;
- the outcome.

In competency-based interviews, you need to demonstrate that you used the skill in a rational way.

Example question and answer

Q: Please tell me about an example of how your academic study has pre-pared you for a career with our company?

A: From reading the job requirements, I see that you want someone who can work independently and take initiative. To produce my dissertation, I had to come up with my own idea for a workable research topic and question, develop a plan for how I would carry out my research and the tasks I needed to do to complete it successfully in the timescale. I showed that I could sustain my focus over many months to deliver a quality piece of work and also when and how to use support from my supervisor.

Interviewers may also ask a question that deals specifically with your dissertation, for example: 'Tell me about your dissertation/project?' When you answer questions such as these, you should be aware of your audience. If your interviewer does not have background knowledge of your subject, do not get too technical in your explanations. Instead, talk about the skills you have demonstrated. You could focus on how you:

- chose your topic area;
- scheduled your time;
- found information;
- conducted the research;
- dealt with problems.

You should also talk about the positive findings that came out of the project, what implications those findings have and what you have learnt from the process of doing the dissertation.

During the recent recruitment of Research Officers, candidates were asked to give a ten-minute presentation to illustrate how their own knowledge and skills met the job description. A number of candidates focused their presentation on the research they had conducted for their university dissertation, discussing the aims, methodology and outcomes. Candidates were asked to suggest what they might have done differently and why, and often discussed their perceptions of the limitations of their research study, resulting from small sample sizes and budgets. By reflecting on their university dissertation, the interview panel had an excellent insight into the knowledge and skills the candidate would bring to the role.

Applications for more advanced levels of study

The research opportunity provided by your dissertation may have led you to consider undertaking further academic study at a higher level. The dissertation might well have sparked a real interest in an area of work that you want to develop further, or you might equally be keen to learn about different approaches to conducting research. You may then be looking for Masters or PhD programmes. If this is the case, then, in your application statement, you will need to emphasize your interest and experience of scholarly activity – your dissertation offers a way of evidencing this and supporting a statement. This will be further helped by a reference from your dissertation supervisor.

> You might build on your dissertation as a Masters project. We have a graduate from the Sheffield Hallam Hong Kong social science programme who has done just that. He is currently enrolled on a Masters programme at City University in Hong Kong where his Masters dissertation (which has extended his undergraduate work) has won him a prize!

Disseminating your research

Having invested so much time in your dissertation, you may wish to consider disseminating your work more widely than the formal assessment document, particularly if you are interested in a career or further studies in academia. Your research may be relatively modest but have some interest to others beyond those marking it.

First you might want to, or already made a commitment to, sharing your findings with research participants and others who supported your research, for example, if you undertook an organizational case study. You may choose to produce extra copies of the document you submit for assessment. An option that might be more user-friendly and cheaper for you is to produce a short summary report saying what you did, who was involved and what you discovered and/or your key messages. A sheet of between 2–4 sides of A4 would be sufficient in an accessible colour and font type and size. If you want to feed back to younger children or adults with learning disabilities you might choose to use images to make more impact. There might be occasions when production of a podcast or short 'talking head' video may be a more appropriate medium through which to share your research findings – five minutes or so should be long enough.

Resources and information about publishing dissertations are commonly aimed at doctoral thesis level, but undergraduate dissertations do receive some attention. Opportunities may include:

* competitions and scholarships;
* student newsletters;
* conference presentations;
* online journals;
* professional journals.

I've used both of my dissertations since graduation. One of them has been rewritten for publication (because it covered a topic that hadn't been researched before in that way) and the other one I regularly use to check back on writing style, referencing formatting and initial readings for new topics that can then be followed up.

Sometimes conferences may have bursaries for students to enable them to attend. There might be opportunities for co-presenting with a staff or faculty member who is working on the same area.

Despite the problems encountered, the work was very rewarding, and I learnt a lot. The findings from the dissertation supported a successful funding application for the project. This gave added value, which was very rewarding, especially to an undergraduate.

Case study: *Reinvention: A Journal of Undergraduate Research* published by the Reinvention Centre of Excellence in Teaching and Learning at Warwick University

Dissertations can take months to prepare, but, once marked, even the best are buried away in departmental archives perhaps never to be seen again. To remedy this, a number of journals have arisen which publish exclusively undergraduate research. Foremost among those publishing social science papers is the multidisciplinary *Reinvention: A Journal of Undergraduate Research*. *Reinvention* was launched in 2007 to provide an outlet for undergraduate work and to encourage students to think seriously about conducting original research.

Reinvention considers manuscripts from undergraduates in any intellectual discipline. For many students, a dissertation is their first experience of original research and can be a good opportunity to submit work for publication. However, there are differences between assessed work and an academic paper, and changes are often required to prepare work for publication.

In common with more traditional academic journals, all submissions to *Reinvention* undergo a stringent system of double-blind peer review. Because of this, it can be a useful experience for students to submit their dissertation research for publication. This means that each article is anonymized and sent to two established experts in the field of interest. These reviewers suggest improvements to the article and make recommendations to the editor as to whether it is of a publishable standard. At this point, the editorial team make a final decision about the article's suitability for publication. If accepted, authors are invited to revise their submission in line with the reviewers' comments. Students whose manuscripts are sent for review may also learn from feedback, which is invariably more detailed than that found on marked coursework. They may also improve their writing style through the process of editing in line with reviewers' comments.

Undergraduate students stand to gain considerably from publishing their work. First, they can learn much about the process of publication; second, publication as a student can greatly boost applications for postgraduate study. It can also suggest to employers that a candidate worked hard and engaged with their discipline at university. Furthermore, authors gain recognition for their dissertation efforts and have the opportunity to share their findings with a large audience.

Reinvention is freely accessible by over 1.3 billion internet users via www.go.warwick.ac.uk/reinventionjournal.

What if . . . you need to resubmit?

There are many reasons why a dissertation may not reach a pass standard at first submission, and, hopefully, if this is the case for you then you will be given an opportunity to resubmit an improved version that will reach the required level. Of course you will be disappointed if you do not pass, but do not give up. If you need to resubmit, you may want to consider:

• re-reading your dissertation through a self-critical lens – the chances are that the time that has lapsed since submission will have enabled you to identify the areas that can be enhanced and strengthened;

• ask someone else to read it and give you comments;

• arrange to speak with your supervisor as soon as possible and utilize all the support you can from them to plan *what* you need to change, *how* to do this and *when* it should be done by.

You may find it difficult to motivate yourself second time round, so, if possible, arrange regular contact with your supervisor to give yourself milestones to work towards.

Students re-submitting dissertations often need to do one of the following: proofread it more carefully; signpost chapters and summarize at end to guide reader and show they understand how they are developing their argument; be clearer about their research question and how they are answering it; show evidence of some ability to critically analyse material.

Key messages

- Submission need not be the end – even if it feels like it on the day you hand your work in.
- Use your dissertation to help you reflect on the wider transferable skills it helped you develop to support your personal and professional development, including employability.
- Make sure you make the most of all the hard work you have put in to support applications and opportunities related to work or study after you have completed your first degree. The more specific you can be about your achievements the better.
- If your dissertation did not reach a pass mark first time round, do not give up: get the best support you can to keep you motivated and to help you improve the work for a second submission.

Key questions

- What did you learn from doing your dissertation?
- What aspects of the work did you enjoy the most?
- What key skills and knowledge did you acquire?
- How might you use these in further study or job applications?
- Would a publication based on your dissertation enhance your job or further study prospects?
- Do you think your dissertation covered a topic and found some results that would be of interest to others? If yes, why not think about publishing an article based on these?

Further reading

Your institution's careers advisory service may have online materials or printed publications on how to get a job after you graduate, and these may include advice on succeeding in interviews.

Hager, P. and Holland, S. (2006) *Graduate Attributes: Learning and Employability*, Dordrecht: Springer.

Luey, B. (ed.) (2004) *Revising Your Dissertation: Advice from Leading Editors*, Berkeley, Calif.: University of California Press.

References

Association of Internet Researchers (AOIR) (2002) *Ethics Guide*, available online at www.aoir.org/?page_id=54 (accessed 8 October 2008).

Allison, B. and Race, P. (2004) *The Student's Guide to Preparing Dissertation and Theses*, London: RoutledgeFalmer.

American Anthropological Association (2004) 'Statement on Ethnography and Institutional Review Boards', available online at www.aaanet.org/stmts/irb.htm (accessed 10 July 2008).

Ashworth, P., Bannister, P. and Thorne, P. (1997) 'Guilty in Whose Eyes? University Students' Perceptions of Cheating and Plagiarism in Academic Work and Assessment', *Studies in Higher Education*, 22 (2): 187–203.

Banks, M. (2007) *Using Visual Data in Qualitative Research*, London: Sage.

Baptiste, I. (2001) 'Qualitative Data Analysis: Common Phases, Strategic Differences', *Forum Qualitative Sozialforschung* (Forum Qualitative Social Research) (Online Journal), 2 (3). Available online at www.qualitative-research.net/fqs/-fqs-eng.htm (accessed 20 March 2008).

Baum, F., MacDougall, C. and Smith, D. (2006) 'Participatory Action Research', *Journal of Epidemiology and Community Health*, 60 (October): 854–857.

Beissel-Durrant, G. (2004) *A Typology of Research Methods Within the Social Sciences*, National Centre for Research Methods: Southampton.

Bhattacharya, K. (2007) 'Consenting to the Consent Form: What Are the Fixed and Fluid Understandings Between the Researcher and the Researched?', *Qualitative Inquiry*, 13 (8): 1095–1115.

Brannen, J. (2005) *Mixed Methods Research: A Discussion Paper*, Southampton: National Centre for Research Methods.

British Sociological Association Visual Sociology Group (2008) *What is visual sociology?*, available online at www.visualsociology.org.uk/ whatis/index.php (accessed 6 October 2008).

Bryman, A. (2004) *Social Research Methods*, 2nd edn, Oxford: Oxford University Press.

Bryman, A. (2008) *Social Research Methods*, 3rd edn, Oxford: Oxford University Press.

Bryman, A. and Cramer, D. (1990) *Quantitative Data Analysis for Social Scientists*, London: Routledge.

Campbell, R. and Wasco, J. (2000) 'Feminist Approaches to Social Science: Epistemological and Methodological Tenets', *American Journal of Community Psychology*, 28 (6): 773–791.

Chandler, Daniel (1994) 'Semiotics for Beginners', available online at www.aber.ac.uk/media/Documents/S4B (accessed 29 April 2008).

Collis, J. and Hussey, R. (2003) *Business Research*, 2nd edn, Basingstoke: Palgrave Macmillan.

Cooper, T. J., Baturo, A. R. and Harris, L. (1998) 'Scholarly Writing in Mathematics and Science Education Higher Degree Courses', in J. A. Malone, B. Atweh and J. R. Northfield (eds) *Research and Supervision in Mathematics and Science Education*, London: Lawrence Erlbaum Associates, pp. 249–276.

Creswell, J. W. (2003) *Research Design: Qualitative, Quantitative, and Mixed Methods Approaches*, 2nd edn, London: Sage.

Denholm, J., Mcleod, D., Boyes, L. and McCormick, J. (2003) *Higher Education: Higher Ambitions? Graduate Employability in Scotland*, Edinburgh: Critical Thinking, Policy Works, Scottish Council.

Denzin, N. K. and Lincoln, Y. S. (2005) *The Sage Handbook of Qualitative Research*, London: Sage.

Dunne, M., Pryor, J. and Yates, P. (2005) *Becoming a Researcher: A Research Companion for the Social Sciences*, Maidenhead: Open University Press.

Economic and Social Research Council (ESRC) (2005) *Research Ethics Framework*, London: ESRC.

Embree, L. (1997) *Encyclopedia of Phenomenology*, Boston, Mass.: Kluwer Academic Publishers.

Ezzy, D. (2002) *Qualitative Research: Practice and Innovation*, London: Routledge.

Fairclough, N. (2003) *Analysing Discourse: Textual Analysis for Social Research*, London: Routledge.

Francis, R. D. (1999) *A Code of Ethics for Psychologists*, Leicester: BPS Books.

Gash, S. (2000) *Effective Literature Searching for Research*, Aldershot: Gower.

Gee, J. P. (2005) *An Introduction to Discourse Analysis: Theory and Method*, London: Routledge.

Gibbs, G. (2007) *Analysing Qualitative Data*, London: Sage.

Glaser, B. and Strauss, A. (1967) *The Discovery of Grounded Theory: Strategies for Qualitative Research*, London: Weidenfeld & Nicolson.

Gorard, S. (2003) *Quantitative Methods in the Social Science: The Role of Numbers Made Easy*, London: Continuum.

Hart, C. (1998) *Doing a Literature Review*, London: Sage.

Holmes, L., Green, M. and Egan, S. (1998) *Graduates in Smaller Businesses: A Pilot Study*, London: Management.

Hunt, A. (2005) *Doing Your Research Project*, London: Routledge.

International Visual Sociology Association (2008) 'What Is Visual Sociology?' Available online at www.visualsociology.org/about.html (accessed 20 July 2008).

Ivanic, R. and Simpson, J. (1992) 'Who's Who in Academic Writing', in N. Fairclough (ed.) *Critical Language Awareness*, London: Longman, pp. 141–173.

Johnson, P. and Duberley, J. (2000) *Understanding Management Research: An Introduction to Epistemology*, London: Sage.

Kandlbinder, P. and Peseta, T. (2006) *In Supervisors' Words: An Insider's View of Postgraduate Supervision*, Sydney: Institute for Teaching and Learning, University of Sydney.

Lawler, S. (2002) 'Narrative in Social Research', in T. May (ed.) *Qualitative Research in Action*, London: Sage.

Lee, R. (2000) *Unobtrusive Methods in Social Research*, Buckingham: Open University Press.

Lewins, A. and Silver, C. (2007) *Using Software in Qualitative Research: A Step-by-Step Guide*, London: Sage.

Macdonald, K. (1993) 'Using Documents', in N. Gilbert (ed.) *Researching Social Life*, London: Sage, pp. 194–210.

McGill, I. and Brockbank, A. (2004) *The Action Learning Handbook: Powerful Techniques for Education*, London: Routledge.

Miles, M. B. and Huberman, A. M. (1994) *Qualitative Data Analysis*, 2nd edn, London: Sage.

Miller, R. L. and Brewer, J. D. (2003) *The A–Z of Social Research*, London: Sage.

Morse, J. M. (2003) 'Principles of mixed method and multi-method research design', in C. Teddlie and A. Tashakkori (eds) *A Handbook of Mixed Methods in Social and Behavioural Research*. London: Sage, pp. 189–208.

Newman, J. M. (2000) 'Action Research: A Brief Overview', *Forum Qualitative Sozialforschung* (Forum: Qualitative Social Research) (Online Journal), 1 (1). Available online at: www.qualitative-research.net/fqs-texte/1–00/1–00newman-e.htm (accessed 10 July 2008).

North, S. (1987) 'The Practitioners', *The Making of Knowledge in Composition: Portrait of an Emerging Field*, Upper Montclair, NJ: Boynton/Cook Publishers.

Open University (n.d.) 'Ethnography Course Information', available online at http://www3.open.ac.uk/courses/bin/p12.dll?C01eD844 (accessed 20 July 2008).

Pilcher, N. (2007) 'Mainland Chinese Supervisors and UK Supervisors: Experiences and Perceptions of Completing Masters Dissertations', Unpublished PhD Thesis, Heriot-Watt University.

Potter, J. (2004) 'Discourse Analysis as a Way of Analysing Naturally Occurring Talk', in D. Silverman (ed.) *Qualitative Research: Theory, Method and Practice*, London: Sage, pp. 200–221.

Pressle, J. (2006) 'Feminist Research Ethics', in S. Nagy Hesse-Bilber (ed.) *Handbook of Feminist Research*, London: Sage, pp. 515–534.

Prosser, J. (2006) 'Working Paper: Researching with Visual Images: Some Guidance Notes and a Glossary for Beginners', *Real Life Methods*, ESRC National Centre for Research Methods Working Paper series 6/06. Available online at www.ncrm.ac.uk/research/outputs/publications/WorkingPapers/2006/0606_researching_visual_images.pdf (accessed 24 April 2008).

Quality Assurance Agency for Higher Education (n.d.) 'Guidelines for HE Progress Files', available online at www.qaa.ac.uk/academicinfrastructure/progressfiles/guidelines/progfile2001.asp (accessed 20 July 2008).

QAA (2006) 'Enhancement Themes', available online at www.enhancementthemes.ac.uk/themes/employability (accessed 20 July 2008).

Rapley, T. (2007) *Doing Conversation, Discourse and Document Analysis*, London: Sage.

Robson, C. (2007) *How to Do a Research Project: A Guide for Undergraduate Students*, Oxford: Blackwell.

Rudestam, K. E. and Newton, R. R. (2001) *Surviving Your Dissertation: A Comprehensive Guide to Content and Process*, 2nd edn, London: Sage.

Schön, D. (1983) *The Reflective Practitioner*, New York: Basic Books.

Silverman, D. (ed.) (2004) *Qualitative Research: Theory, Method and Practice*, London: Sage.

Silverman, D. (2000) *Doing Qualitative Research: A Practical Handbook*, London: Sage.

Southerton, D. (2002) 'Boundaries of "Us" and "Them": Class, Mobility and Identification in a New Town', *Sociology*, 36 (1): 171–193.

Spencer, S. (2005) *Framing the Fringe Dwellers*, C-SAP Teaching Race and Ethnicity in Higher Education Website, available online at www.teachingrace.bham.ac.uk/video_resources/fringe_dwellers.htm (accessed 4 June 2008).

Spencer, S. (2006) *Race and Ethnicity: Culture, Identity and Representation*, London: Routledge.

Stewart, J. and Knowles, V. (1999) 'The Changing Nature of Graduate Careers', *Career Development International*, 4 (7): 370–383.

Strauss, A. and Corbin, J. (1998) *Basics of Qualitative Research: Techniques and Procedures for Developing Grounded Theory*, 2nd edn, London: Sage.

Sussman, M. and Gilgun, J. F. (1997) *The Methods and Methodologies of Qualitative Family Research*, New York: Haworth Press.

Swales, J. M. and Feak, C. B. (2004) *Academic Writing for Graduate Students: Essential Tasks and Skills*, Ann Arbor, Mich.: University of Michigan Press.

Taylor, G. (1989) *The Students' Writing Guide for the Arts and Social Sciences*, Cambridge: Cambridge University Press.

Todd, M., Bannister, P. and Clegg, S. (2004) 'Independent Inquiry and the Undergraduate Dissertation: Perceptions and Experiences of Final Year Social Science Students', *Assessment and Evaluation in Higher Education*, 29: 335–355.

Todd, M. J., Smith, K. and Bannister, P. (2006) 'Staff Experiences and Perceptions of Supervising a Social Science Undergraduate Dissertation', *Teaching in Higher Education*, 11 (2): 161–173.

Tysick, C. (2004) 'Concept Mapping and the Research Process: A Librarian's Perspective', *Concept Maps: Theory, Methodology, Technology*, Proceedings of the First International Conference on Concept Mapping, Pamplona, Spain. Available online at www.cmc.ihmc.us/papers/cmc2004–20.pdf (accessed 4 February 2008).

Van der Velde, N., Jansen, P. and Anderson, N. (2004) *Guide to Management Research Methods*, Oxford: Blackwell.

Waldman, J. (1999) *Help Yourself to Learning at Work*, Lyme Regis: Russell House.

Walliman, N. S. R. (2004) *Your Undergraduate Dissertation: The Essential Guide for Success*, London: Sage.

Weiss, C. H. (1998) *Evaluation: Methods for Studying Programs and Policies*, 2nd edn, Upper Saddle River, NJ: Prentice Hall.

Wiles, R., Heath, S., Crow, G. and Charles, V. (2005) *Informed Consent in Social Research: A Literature Review*, Southampton: National Centre for Research Methods.

Wilkinson, S. (2004) 'Focus Group Research', in Silverman, D. (ed.) *Qualitative Research: Theory, Method and Practice*, London: Sage.

World Medical Association (WMA) (2004) 'Declaration of Helsinki', available online at www.wma.net/e/ethicsunit/helsinki.htm (accessed 20 July 2008).

Index